Kiln Construction

A Brick by Brick Approach

Kiln Construction

A Brick by Brick Approach

Joe Finch

HERBERT PRESS
LONDON • OXFORD • NEW YORK • NEW DELHI • SYDNEY

University of Pennsylvania Press • Philadelphia

Frontispiece *Large plate by Joe Finch, dia: 37cm (14 1/2in.), raw glazed and fired in a wood kiln.*

HERBERT PRESS
Bloomsbury Publishing Plc
50 Bedford Square, London, WC1B 3DP, UK
29 Earlsfort Terrace, Dublin 2, Ireland

BLOOMSBURY, HERBERT PRESS and the Herbert Press logo are trademarks of Bloomsbury Publishing Plc

First published in Great Britain in 2006 by
A&C Black Publishers Limited
This edition published in 2024

Published simultaneously in the USA by
University of Pennsylvania Press
3905 Spruce Street
Philadelphia, Pennsylvania 19104-4112
www.pennpress.org

A catalogue record for this book is available from the British Library

UK ISBN: 978-1-789943-51-1
US ISBN: 978-1-512827-22-4

2 4 6 8 10 9 7 5 3 1

Book design by Susan McIntyre
Cover design by Peter Bailey
Printed and bound in China by C&C Offset Printing Co., Ltd.

MIX
Paper | Supporting responsible forestry
FSC® C008047

Cover illustrations

Front (background) Stoking the firebox; (top) Cutting through HTIs; (middle) Early stages of kiln, showing firebars in positio (bottom) Scotland in the snow.

Back (top) Packing the wood kiln; (middle) Building a kiln in India; (bottom) Stoking the wood kiln.

Contents

Dedication

I wish to dedicate this book to my father Ray Finch who set me off on this wonderful adventure of being a potter. His help and advice over the years has been invaluable and his life and work an inspiration to me.

Ray throwing a teapot.

Acknowledgements

With thanks to my wife Trudi, for helping me fire and for putting up with my kiln obsession. Also thanks to David Gardner for his brilliant diagrams and drawings of my kilns.

Supported by the Arts Council of Wales.

CEFNOGI CREADIGRWYDD
CYNGOR CELFYDDYDAU CYMRU
THE ARTS COUNCIL OF WALES
SUPPORTING CREATIVITY

Foreword by Frederick Olsen

Like roaring infernos, all kilns command the potter's environment. They hold us captive, leaving us half fearing the outcome while anticipating what wonderful manifestations could occur. Kilns play a major role in a potter's ceramic life. They become icons associated with one's work; they are stars of many slide shows; they become a symbol of a potter's wealth; and hold the outcome of our work in their cooling chamber. Considered both creator and annihilator of the potter's ceramic realm; praised for the resulting ceramic art produced and denounced as rapacious consumers of energy and producers of pollutants.

For thirty years potters have asked me for complete plans for my Olsen Fastfire down-draught kiln design and I have always replied that what is in *The Kiln Book* is all I have, and it seemed to be enough since this kiln design has become one of the world's most popularly built kilns. Now I can inform people of a brand new book on how to build a modified Fastfire kiln design, called *Kiln Construction, a Brick by Brick Approach.*

Years ago Joe sent me a series of slides on his modifications to the exit flue channel which was a logical and practical alteration. I was happy to know someone was taking the design to the next level. He has perfected other alterations to the basic construction in this book and has demonstrated it all very well. His step-by-step method is illustrated with remarkable computer-generated graphics to go alongside the photographic documentation of each stage. One thing I am very impressed by is that his design is a true down-draught. Another feature of the basic design is that it can be altered to fire using all wood, a combination of wood and gas, all gas, or oil just by changing the initial floor plan. His book gives all three alterations in step-by-step construction details.

The book's superb photographs and graphics lead to excellent communication between the author and reader. It will give the reader and beginner kiln-builder the courage and knowledge to build their first kiln successfully.

Joe's three designs have been proven by the test of time and fired by many satisfied potters. My congratulations to Joe and his book will be a must for my library.

Frederick Olsen

Preface

There are a great number of books covering all the various aspects of pottery and ceramics but very few on the subject of kilns, to my knowledge only five. These books contain much detailed and valuable information, and although I would recommend them to anyone wanting to know about kilns, I don't consider they give sufficient information on any tried and proven kiln that would enable someone without kiln building experience to build and fire their own kiln. In this book I do not try to cover the vast array of different kilns but rather concentrate on a few designs that I have developed, built and fired successfully – kilns that are easy to build and fire.

This book hopefully will dispel the concerns that many people have over kiln building and give them the confidence to go ahead and build their own kiln, thus saving money and giving themselves great satisfaction and a better understanding of the workings of a kiln.

Included in this book are:

- Detailed information and step-by-step instructions on how to build tried and tested kilns.
- Full plans and colour photographs showing brick by brick construction.
- Description and lists of materials and tools needed for the construction.
- Practical advice on kiln setting and firing schedules.

Introduction

You cannot be a potter or ceramicist if you are unable to fire the items you produce. Although you can fire clay without a kiln, in a bonfire or pit, it is not a practical option for 99% of potters. Therefore the one piece of equipment every potter must have access to is a kiln.

Bonfire firing at Aberystwyth International Ceramics Festival 2005.
PHOTO EDDIE DOUGHTON

Although it isn't essential to own the kiln you use and many people do fire their work at schools, colleges, institutions, in a shared workshop or through pottery friends, it can prove difficult fitting in with other people's timetable and firing requirements. If you produce work on a regular basis it is probably time you considered having your own kiln.

A new kiln purchased from a manufacturer or pottery supplier is an expensive item. In fact it is probably the most costly single item a potter needs. Substantial savings can be made if you are willing and able to build your own kiln but many potters are too apprehensive to take this step, fearful that they do not have the technical knowledge or skills necessary to construct this indispensable item.

Ray Finch throwing in 2005. PHOTO MIKE FINCH.

The purpose of this book is to give detailed information, plans and step-by-step instructions for kilns that I've tried and tested to allow those who wish to build their own kiln to proceed, confident that they can be successful in this endeavour. However, although I have included details on setting and firing the kilns and have had many successful firings in them, there can be no guarantee that any firing will be the total success you may be hoping for. All potters can cite occasions when they have experienced problems with firings that have not been the fault of the kiln but of the weather, the fuel or the human operator! With so many variables affecting a firing, trial and error are still likely to be the stepping-stones to experience and success.

As a full time potter, and one that has made a living from pottery for over forty years, it has always been essential that I have had a reliable and economic kiln. I was fortunate to be born the son of master potter Ray Finch, who started potting in 1936 under Michael Cardew. (As I write this, Ray is still making and exhibiting wonderful pots at the age of 91.)

Being raised and taught at Winchcombe Pottery, alongside a number of skilled potters, ensured that from an early age I experienced a wonderful training. Part of this training included the experience of kiln building, when I learnt first hand the basics of kiln design. This was to stand me in good stead when, at the age of 22, I was employed to establish the first studio pottery in Lesotho (Southern Africa) and had to design and build a 60cu. ft. (1.7m^3) oil-fired kiln.

Kiln building is a subject that has always fascinated me and over the years I have built numerous kilns of different size and fuel type for myself and other potters. My favourite kiln is the 60cu. ft. (1.7m^3) wood-fired kiln, featured in this book, that I have developed and used for many years now. I have built this design for potters in Scotland, Wales, England, Ireland and India and demonstrated how to build and fire it at the fifth International Ceramic Festival held at Aberystwyth, Wales in 1995.

Scotland in the snow.

Thomastown, Eire.

Cumbria, England.

India in the sun.

A pot enveloped in flames while being fired in a gas kiln.

Chapter 1

What Kiln to Build?

A simple definition of a pottery kiln is a structure that can retain enough of the heat introduced into it to fire clay. (Peter Lange, a New Zealand potter, has demonstrated firing a 'kiln' built of ice. Although most people would prefer their kiln to last more than twenty minutes!).

Clay is 'fired' when it is heated above a point where an irreversible change occurs. The chemically combined water is driven off, altering the clay's composition, so that it will not disintegrate in water or return to its plastic state. That first irreversible change, which happens at about 600°C (1112°F), is just the start of a series of changes that clay goes through as it is heated. It will change colour, become harder, shrink and if taken high enough, will vitrify and finally melt.

It is easy to build a kiln to fire at low temperatures. A 30cm (12in.) tin or metal dustbin could be described as a kiln when being used to sawdust fire pots, as it should reach 700°C (1292°F) or more. A raku kiln that fires to 1000°C (1832°F) can be quickly

'Ice kiln' *fired by Peter Lange.* PHOTO EDDIE DOUGHTON.

constructed using ceramic fibre inside a metal dustbin or a simple brick construction. However, the higher the temperature you are aiming for the more important the design and construction of the kiln becomes. Controlling the temperature rise, retaining the heat with insulation, reducing heat loss via the exit flue or chimney and acquiring an even temperature throughout the firing chamber becomes increasingly essential for an efficient kiln.

When planning to build a kiln there are a number of decisions you need to make:

- *What type of pottery do you want to make?*
- *To what temperature do you wish to fire?*
- *What size of kiln and how often do you intend to fire?*
- *What fuel will it use?*
- *What atmosphere and draught type will it have?*
- *Are you looking for special effects? Ash, salt, soda, crystal, lustre?*
- *Where are you going to locate the kiln?*

What type of pottery do you want to make and to what temperature are you planning to fire?

Earthenware or slipware is fired between 900°C and 1150°C (1652°F and 2102°F) and stoneware in the region of 1200°C (2192°F) to 1320°C (2408°F). The higher the temperature you fire, the more expensive the kiln is likely to be as the materials will need to be better quality and thus more costly. The firing time and fuel costs will also increase dramatically as the temperatures rises, especially above 1100°C (2012°F).

All kilns described in this book could be used for earthenware or stoneware (depending on the materials used). However, a kiln built of refractories capable of firing to stoneware temperatures can always be fired lower but a kiln built of materials to fire at 1150°C (2102°F) would not be suitable, or safe, to fire at 1300°C (2372°F). If you are only planning to fire earthenware it may be better to use an electric kiln as they are relatively inexpensive to fire, easy to use, efficient, reliable, and fire with an oxidising atmosphere, which is generally what is needed for earthenware. Do check that the power supply is sufficient for the size of kiln you want as installing a larger supply or three-phase can be expensive. I am not including any designs or plans for building an electric kiln.

If you want to produce reduction fired stoneware, lustre or to salt or soda fire then, a 'flame' kiln burning natural gas, propane (LPG), oil or wood, built with good quality refractory materials, should be your choice.

What size of kiln and how often do you intend to fire?

The size of the kiln may be dictated by the space available but, if this is not a limitation, then there are various other considerations.

A 40cm (15¾in.) diameter pot will require a shelf approximately 50 x 35cm (19¾ x 13¾in.) to allow for props.

How frequently do you wish to fire? Some potters are happy to fire only three or four times a year, whereas others fire twice a week. The type of kiln you have may dictate the frequency of firing. With an electric or gas kiln, with a controller to program your firing cycle, you could easily fire two or three times a week. Many potters find this an advantage as they use the heat from the regular firings to heat their workshop and dry their pots. If you are firing by gas or oil with manual burners and controls, you would probably not wish to fire more than once a week due to the time attending to the kiln. On the other hand, if you are firing with wood, then a three to six week cycle is most likely to suit you best as the effort and time involved in wood firing makes it less suitable for more frequent use.

What size of work do you produce and in what volume? This obviously relates to the above paragraph but if you plan to produce even a few large diameter pots you need to ensure the kiln shelves are sufficient in size, allowing for shrinkage and the space the kiln props take, to accommodate your work. I realise this is stating the obvious but it is surprising how easy it is to overlook these simple points with the excitement of designing your new kiln.

Do you already have kiln shelves? Are they the weight and size you are happy to work with? If so you may want to design the kiln to fit the shelves you have and save the expense of buying new ones. It is worth bearing in mind that the kiln shelves are a percentage (albeit small) of the total cost of the kiln and that, if looked after properly, can last for hundreds of firings. For this reason it is more important that you design the kiln to fit the ideal shelf size for you. Look into the possibility of purchasing the modern thinner shelves that are lighter if you require a large size. Don't be tempted to purchase a shelf size that will be too heavy or difficult for you to lift into those awkward parts of the kiln. Check the weight before you buy and finalise your kiln design.

Some people have the problem that they need a large kiln to accommodate the size of work they wish to produce but their output is slow. In a situation like this, the case of sharing a kiln should be considered. I said earlier it can prove difficult fitting in with other peoples' timetable and firing requirements but sharing a kiln with a small group of like-minded potters can work to everyone's advantage. The cost of the kiln and fuel can be split between the group and the packing and firing of the kiln is often an easier and more enjoyable task when shared.

An example of this working well is a group of potters in Ireland who all have their own studios and kilns firing with gas, oil or electricity but all wanted to do some wood fired pottery. They decided to form a wood firing group which has proved not only cost effective but firings have become a social event. They have even taken it a step further by organising group exhibitions of work from the kiln.

What fuel will fire your kiln?

The design of your kiln will vary according to the type of fuel you use. Electricity needs no fireboxes, flues or chimney, whereas oil and gas need all of these and if you intend to fire with wood the fireboxes, flues and chimney need to be substantially larger than for a gas- or oil-fired kiln.

In this book I am concentrating on 'flame' fired kilns using gas, oil and wood and do not feature building an electric kiln. This is not because there is anything wrong with electric kilns or that it is impossible to build your own but rather that there are many very good electric kilns available, either new or second hand, so building your own is unlikely to be practical. (Remember an electric kiln fires with an oxidising atmosphere and do check your power supply is sufficient for the size of kiln you want before purchasing.)

If you have mains gas already connected to your property this is likely to be your best option of fuel to fire your kiln as it is probably the cheapest and most convenient of the 'flame' fuels. However do find out from your gas supplier if the supply will be sufficient for your needs. If the gas pipe to your property is too small, check on the cost of installing a suitable supply. Gas burners are easy to operate and with 'fail-safe' devices fitted to them, the burners are safe to use. Mains gas also has the advantage of being quiet to fire and produces no smoke to annoy neighbours, even when reducing.

Without the option of mains gas, oil, LPG (Liquified Petroleum Gas) or wood are alternative choices, each of which have their own pros and cons.

Oil pros:

- At the time of writing this book, oil was on a par with mains gas for cost as fuel.
- You may already have an oil tank that you use for heating the house or workshop and be happy for this to serve the kiln as well, thus saving the cost of purchasing another tank.
- Another option could be to use waste vegetable or engine oil and 'drip plate' burners, saving on the cost of burners and air blower. Although waste oil is cheap and sometimes free, the time and effort needed to collect, possibly filter and store the oil need to be considered. Also, you should contact the Environmental Agency to see if you need a licence to collect, store and burn waste oil.

Oil cons:

- Oil can produce smoke and fumes when reducing.
- Apart from 'drip plate' burners, oil burners need a forced air supply from a fan.
- Oil fumes can be dirty and smelly.

LPG pros:

- LPG can be delivered in gas bottles, which have the advantage of being portable and may be essential if the kiln is built in an inaccessible site; or delivered by tanker and stored in a bulk tank. Again you may already have a tank that could also serve the kiln.
- There are many LPG burners that work on the pressure of gas and do not need a forced air supply. (This may be important if the kiln site is without power.)
- Gas burners are easy to operate and with 'fail-safe' devices fitted, they are also safe to use.
- No smoke is produced when firing.
- LPG requires the smallest flues and chimneys of all the 'flame' kilns.

LPG cons:

- LPG is probably the most expensive fuel to use, especially if you are using bottles rather than a bulk tank.

Wood pros:

- The ash effects you can achieve using wood as a fuel can be very exciting, decorative and aesthetically pleasing.
- It should be a cheap fuel if you find a local supply of suitable waste wood.
- Wood firing can satisfy one's pyromaniac tendencies!

Wood cons:

- A lot of time and labour is spent cutting, stacking and stoking.
- Large, dry store areas are needed to stockpile the kiln wood as it has to be seasoned and completely dry.
- Suitable wood for firing can be difficult to locate. You may be lucky and find kiln-dried off cuts from some local factory, but if you are buying waste wood from a sawmill it may need to be stored for a year before it is ready to burn.
- Undesirable smoke may be produced when firing with wood.

What atmosphere and draught type?

The kiln needs to be able to fire with an oxidised or reduced atmosphere and if designed properly this should not be a problem.

The three types of 'flame' kilns are described as: up-draught, cross-draught and down-draught (see opposite).

The kilns described in detail in this book are all down-draught – as in my opinion they fire more evenly and are the most efficient.

Do you require special effects?

Different results can be created within the kiln during firing. For example the introduction of sodium to produce salt or soda glaze, fly-ash from wood firing generating those subtle flashes of colour, cooling procedures that create crystalline glazes, reducing lustres and of course the effects of reduction or oxidation. To achieve these different results it may be necessary to modify the design of your kiln. Although this is not a book about salt, soda, crystalline or lustre firings, since others have covered those subjects fully, I will touch only briefly on them to show how they may influence kiln design. A soda and a wood-fired kiln are two of the kiln designs that feature later in the book.

Salt-glaze entails introducing salt (NaCl) into the kiln towards the end of the firing, when the heat will decompose and vaporise it, producing sodium chloride vapour. This

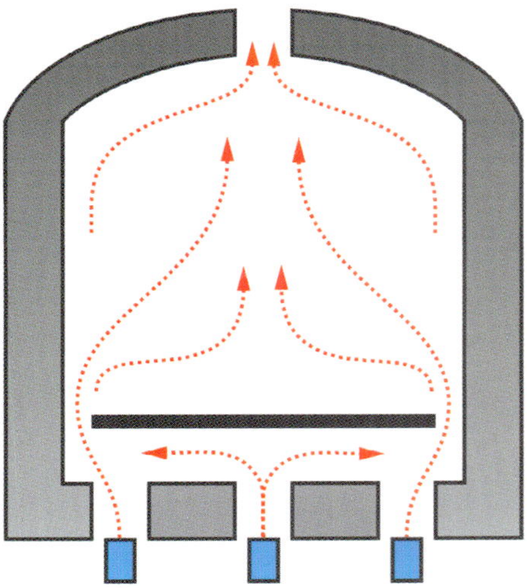

Up-draught kiln with burners below floor level.

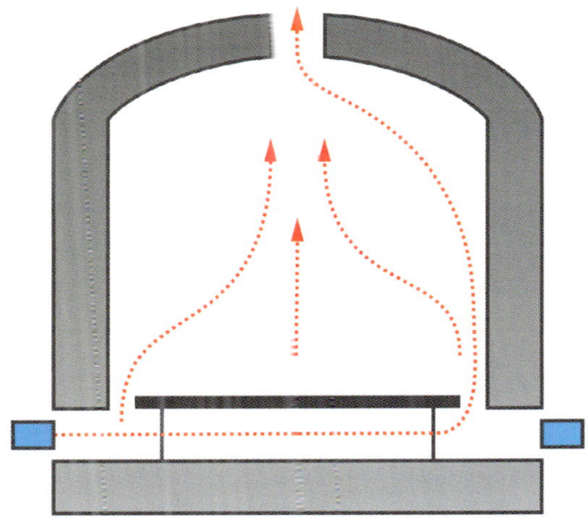

Up-draught kiln with burners entering at floor level.

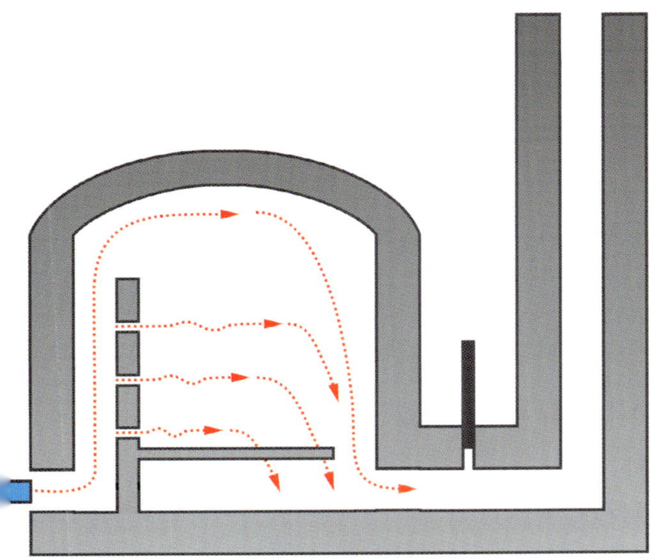

Cross-draught kiln.

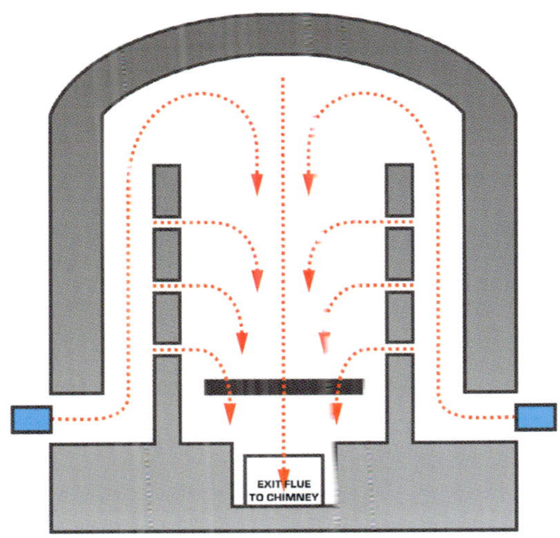

Down-draught kiln.

Ruthanne Tudball spraying soda solution into kiln. Note the use of gloves and goggles.

gas, which contains soda and is a flux, will react with the alumina and silica in the clay and slip to produce sodium alumina silicate, which in turn is a glaze.

None of the kiln designs in this book are really suitable for salt-glazing due to the use of both soft bricks internally and ceramic firebars, as the salt will quickly erode them. This could be remedied by using metal firebars and hard bricks internally. Three main considerations in designing and building a salt-glaze kiln however, are:

- How you intend to introduce the salt into the kiln.
- How you protect the kiln from the corrosive nature of sodium chloride.
- How you efficiently and safely ventilate the kiln and area around it from the potentially hazardous sodium chloride vapour. This is a toxic vapour that has a damaging effect on metal and inhaling the fumes must be avoided as it could damage your lungs.

Pollution laws are likely to preclude salt firing, especially in urban areas.

Soda firing, which also relies on sodium vapour to create the sodium silicate glaze, has the advantage of not producing the harmful dilute hydrochloride acid vapour as a by-product, so may be used to fire in some urban environments. It also tends to be less corrosive on the kiln and kiln furniture but effective ways of introducing the soda still need to be designed into the kiln. If a solution of soda is to be sprayed into the kiln, enough spy holes need to be made to allow sufficient coverage to all parts of the kiln.

Should the intention be to add the soda by painting it onto wood (heated soda crystals become liquid), then stoke-holes and fire bars will need to be provided.

If you wish to produce crystalline glazes, which contain crystals within and on the surface of the glaze it is vital to have a kiln that you can control and hold the temperature during the cooling period. It is then that the essential oxides are isolated from the still fluid glaze in a process called devitrification. Holding the kiln temperature at about 800°C (1472°F) encourages and allows the crystals to grow. Electric kilns are ideal for this, especially if you are able to program the cooling rate, although you would be firing in an oxidised atmosphere. Gas or oil could also be used and would give you the choice of reduction firing but again it would be desirable to have an automatic temperature control that would work during cooling. Although, in theory, you can produce crystalline glaze effects in a wood-fired kiln it would be difficult and tiring to achieve.

Flame kilns are the easiest for producing lustre, as to create metallic surfaces on the glazes requires a reduction atmosphere within the kiln to convert the oxide or resinate to the pure metal. However, it is possible to convert an electric kiln so that gas is introduced creating the reduction process needed for lustre (although this is both more difficult and somewhat hazardous!). Jonathan Chiswell Jones, well known for his beautifully decorated lustreware, employs this method.

Autumn Leaves bowl, *dia: 15cm (6in.), silver lustre, and* Cockerel bowl, *dia: 18cm (7in.), silver and copper lustre. Both by Jonathan Chiswell Jones.*

Chapter 2

Location

The location of your kiln is an important factor and should be given due consideration. The five main points you need to consider are: convenience, cover, neighbours, planning and safety. (Listed alphabetically and not necessarily in importance.)

Convenience It is desirable to have the kiln near the studio where the pots are made but depending on the type of kiln and the ventilation system installed it is proabably best if the kiln is not located in the workshop where you could be affected by fumes, smoke, soot, noise and unwanted heat. There are potters who fire their electric or gas kilns within their workshop and rely on the waste heat to warm the workshop and dry their pots, but I must stress the importance of adequate ventilation as even an electric kiln will give off fumes during the firing of the ware. It would be unwise to locate an oil or wood-fired kiln within your workshop due to the fumes, smoke and soot produced, especially if you are reduction firing.

When choosing the site for the kiln, do consider how you will get your chosen fuel to the kiln. A potter I know has to wheel large propane cylinders through her house to get to the kiln shed. Not an ideal situation! If you are wanting to have wood delivered, you will need to consider ease of access and storage. Also worth considering is that even if your kiln does not require electricity, a safe supply will be of great assistance. Lights, extractor-fan, and power for a pyrometer, are just three examples of the benefits.

Cover It is most unpleasant to pack and fire a kiln in the wind and rain. The kiln is also vulnerable – ceramic fibre and insulating bricks soak up water like a sponge and to dry out a wet kiln will use a considerable amount of extra fuel, the firing will take longer, and will be more costly than firing a dry kiln. So in order to protect the kiln and yourself when packing and firing it is advisable to have some sort of cover over the kiln. If you have an existing outhouse, shed or garage you may decide to build your kiln there but you must check the fumes and fire hazards (see Chapter 3). If you are

Ruthanne Tudball's kiln room, separate but next to her workshop, located under an open-plan roofed structure.

thinking of firing with wood you will need a large covered area near the kiln to store your dry wood.

Neighbours The position of the kiln could adversely affect you and your neighbours if they live close by. If possible site the kiln so the prevailing wind will disperse any smoke, noise and fumes away from habitation or work places (I have always been fortunate to live and work in the country where any activity impinges less on others). It is important to keep up good relations with your neighbours so I would suggest discussing your plans with them at an early stage. It may be a good idea to try to involve them in some way, perhaps by letting them make a few pots and promising to fire them in the new kiln!

Wooden beam over kiln arch being covered with ceramic fibre and tin foil as a safety measure.

Planning Although I have never found it necessary to have planning permission for any of the kilns I have built, it would be advisable to seek the advice of the local planning department. If you intend to build a structure to put the kiln in you might find that, although the kiln does not require planning permission, the kiln shed/room does. (I feel personally that the kiln itself should not require planning permission, especially if it is made without mortar or foundations – but the planning department may disagree!)

Remember you should inform your insurance company where you plan to locate the kiln. Your first choice may have a significant effect on your premiums, while another position may be totally acceptable to them. If you don't tell your insurance company and have the misfortune to have a fire, which could spread to another property compounding the problem, you may not be covered.

Safety The question of safety and the location of the kiln should be your primary concern. Ensure that any smoke, fumes, heat or fire from the kiln cannot cause damage to people or property. Combustible material should be kept at a safe distance from the kiln and chimney, and if firing in an enclosed area ventilation must be provided.

Two other points that should be checked and considered when deciding on the location are:

Is the site free from the dangers of flooding? As long as this is only likely to be a rare occurence and the maximum depth not to exceed 10cm (4in.), building the kiln on hollow concrete blocks should minimise the problem.

Can the site be made secure? A kiln with its shelves, props, pyrometer, etc. is an expensive and valuable item and with its fuel source, should not be a playground for the local children.

Chapter 3

Health and Safety

Fire risk A few potters have had serious fires, some have had small fires or close calls but the majority with careful thought, planning and attention to safety have had no problems. The local fire officer is usually happy to come and advise on precautions you may need to take. Fire extinguishers of the appropriate type or, in the case of oil-fired kilns, buckets of sand should be placed close at hand in case of any fire starting outside the kiln.

The kiln, if built properly, should not in itself be a fire hazard. After all it is designed and built to keep the heat in. When fires involving kilns have started it is usually because the kiln has been built too close to a roof timber or other combustible material. I would recommend having a minimum of 1m (3⅓ft) clearance and if possible using non-combustible building materials in the vicinity of the kiln.

Check for cracks in the kiln, especially as it ages, as flame and heat escaping could become a danger that was not present when the kiln was new.

Another danger point is the exit flue and chimney, especially if the chimney is to go through the roof. Also, make sure there are no overhanging trees or vegetation too close and periodically cut back any greenery too close to the chimney.

It is worth noting that a number of serious fires involving kilns have happened while the kiln was unattended, often after the firing finished. This is because when a kiln is clammed-up at the end of the firing and the exit flues and chimney are closed off, the massive amount of heat remaining in the kiln still needs to discharge. The temperature of the exterior of the kiln will increase greatly during this initial cooling stage so it is most important that, at the end of the firing, you clear around the kiln and make sure no combustible material is left within 1m (3⅓ft) of it.

Fumes Fumes from kilns can be poisonous, smelly and dirty. It is essential to install an efficient system of evacuating any fumes that may be created around the kiln area. Adequate natural draught ventilation should be designed into the building as both kilns and those who fire them need to breathe! It is not advisable to rely solely on an extractor fan because a power cut or failure during firing could result in a dangerous build up of fumes. The kiln chimney needs to be high enough and of the correct proportion to disperse the smoke and vapours away from the kiln.

Carbon monoxide, which is produced when a reduction atmosphere is achieved, is deadly poisonous and especially dangerous because you cannot see or smell it.

The white vapour fumes created when 'salt firing' were considered to be dilute hydrochloric acid vapour, but recent research suggests this is not the case and that the fumes are a saline vapour. Even so, inhaling the fumes should be avoided.

Gas and oil fumes can have an unpleasant smell and although I consider smoke from a wood-fired kiln acceptable not everyone will be of the same opinion. Washing which smells of bonfires, is probably something only potters will tolerate! Both oil and wood firing usually produce smoke during reduction.

Dust and fibres Many ceramic materials contain silica. If this becomes airborne as fine dust of less than 5 microns it can be taken into the lungs and will remain there. If dust is inhaled over a long period it can cause silicosis. Although the studio potter is not at special risk, breathing in dust should be guarded against. When undertaking any action that produces dust, whether cutting, drilling or rubbing-down bricks, always wear a mask/respirator. It is especially important to wear a respirator and suitable gloves and clothing when working with ceramic fibre, as tiny fibres can be inhaled and are considered carcinogenic.

Burns and injuries When building and firing a kiln, care and the correct clothing will minimise the risk of any injury. Suitable gloves, clothing, footwear and eye protection need to be worn. Children should not be allowed near the kiln during firing as the exterior of even a well-insulated kiln could inflict burns if touched.

If firing with gas or oil much less protection is needed than if stoking with wood. But at top temperatures removing a spy hole brick or altering a damper will necessitate the use of gloves, and welders' glasses or goggles should be used to prevent retinal damage when looking into a kiln at high temperatures. Normal sunglasses are inadequate.

Wood firing presents many more dangers. Before you fire, start cutting and moving the wood. If using a chain saw the correct clothing and procedures must be followed. Safety glasses and suitable gloves should be worn when moving wood to prevent the risk of splinters. When stoking, cotton or wool garments are best as they provide better insulation to the wearer than synthetic fabrics, which can ignite and melt at temperatures far lower than natural fibres. Long sleeve shirts and long trousers are advisable and some people wear a leather apron as extra protection. Gloves should be worn when stoking and I find that welders' gauntlets give an extra defence from the heat. Sturdy shoes or work-boots should be worn when moving wood or firing. A clear walk-way around the kiln should be maintained while firing to minimise the risk of tripping or stepping on anything hot or sharp.

Leaks If using gas or oil as your fuel you must ensure that there are no leaks. Check all gas joints with soapy water. (Bubbles will be visible if there is a leak.) Remember that propane and butane are heavier than air and leaking gas would drop to the floor and pool at the lowest point whereas natural gas is lighter than air and could accumulate in roof areas. Both could build up to a point when an explosion could occur.

Chapter 4

Materials

There are many different materials that can be utilized in kiln building. But, for the purpose of this book, I will only describe the items that are incorporated in the illustrated kilns and are commonly used.

Various types of bricks are used each with their own properties and advantages. In the UK the firebricks and insulating bricks measure 23 × 11.5 × 7.6cm (9in. × 4½in. × 3in.). Common house bricks vary in size depending on the manufacturer but are usually smaller than the insulating ones and firebricks. The ones I have used measure 21.5 × 10 × 6.4cm (8½in. × 4in. × 2½in.).

Firebricks Sometimes referred to as 'heavies' because they weigh about 3.5kg (8lbs), are strong and dense but are poor insulators and absorb a lot of heat. It is reckoned that a kiln built just of firebricks would use approximately four times the amount of fuel compared to the same kiln built with insulating bricks. Firebricks are generally used in the base of the kiln where their strength is needed to support the weight of the pots, shelves, and props and in the fireboxes to protect against the ravages of intense heat, abrasion, spalling and the corrosive effects of ash, salt or soda. Cutting firebricks is hard work and they are usually broken with the use of a 'lump hammer' and bolster. The job of breaking the brick will be much easier if you score the brick first with a stone cutting disk in an electric hand-held grinder – goggles and mask must be worn. It is a great advantage if you can design your kiln so that the number of cut bricks is kept to a minimum.

Firebrick.

HTI brick 26 grade.

Identification number	Recommended top temp. °F	Recommended top temp. °C	Main usage in kiln construction
20	2000°F	1095°C	As a back up brick
23	2300°F	1260°C	For kilns not exceeding cone 7
26	2600°F	1425°C	An excellent brick for kilns firing to cone 13
28	2800°F	1535°C	Only needed for extreme temperature areas

Insulating bricks Sometimes called hot face insulating bricks or insulating fire bricks. Available in a range of grades designated by different numbers refering to their temperature capability in Fahrenheit (see table above). They are lighter than firebricks, much better insulators and easily cut with a saw. I would recommend the '26 grade' for building the chamber walls and arch for a kiln firing to stoneware temperatures, especially if you intend to fire to 1300°C (2372°F) or over.

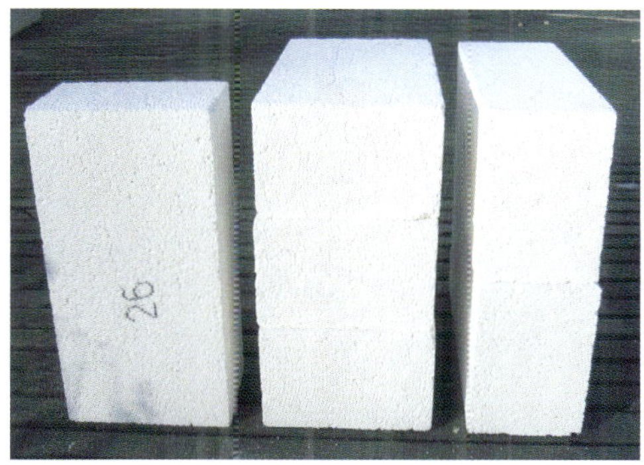

1 brick on end = 3 flat = 2 on their side.

Arch bricks There are two main types of arch bricks, side arch and end arch. I always use side arch bricks and back up with ceramic fibre or other insulating material. They are quicker to lay, use half the number compared to end arch bricks, so saving half the cost, and they make a strong and safe arch. Refractory brick companies can supply arch bricks that are cut exactly and for the extra small amount they charge make it not worth cutting your own.

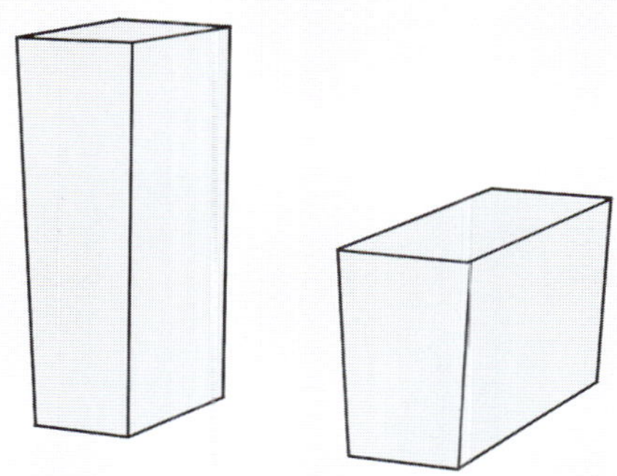

LEFT *End arch brick.* RIGHT *Side arch brick.*

Common house bricks These are the fired clay ones as opposed to the composite cement brick, and can be used for building the upper part of the chimney. I usually recommend that approximately the first 1m (3⅓ft) is built out of firebricks but after that 'commons' are fine. They will have been fired to 900°C (1652°F) or more and if your chimney is getting to that temperature you are wasting a lot of heat. Some builders merchants sell a fired brick that is light yellow in colour, much like firebricks.

(Ibstock Brick Company near Bristol produce a brick called 'Gloucester Gold', these are akin to firebricks and tests have shown that they will fire to over 1100°C/2012°F, so would be ideal for building the chimney.)

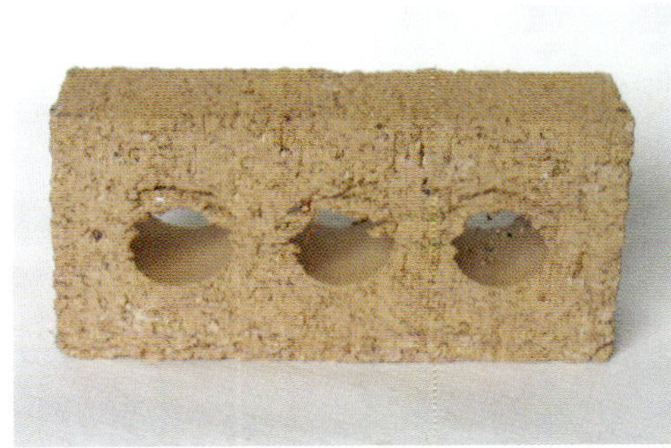

Gloucester Gold brick.

Concrete blocks Like common house bricks, these can be purchased from your local builders merchant. The ones I use are the hollow blocks measuring 43.7 × 21.7 × 21.7cm (17¼ × 8½ × 8½in.) and are useful for a number of reasons:

- they insulate and prevent heat damage to the ground or floor under the kiln;
- they raise the level, making packing and firing more comfortable;
- they can help prevent moisture rising into the kiln if your kiln site is prone to damp.

I only use concrete blocks as a foundation layer and recommend that they are protected from excessive heat with ceramic fibre or firebricks.

Mortar You can purchase various ceramic mortars or you can mix your own using fireclay, sand and water. However, if you are buying new bricks I would suggest that you don't use any mortar. Occasionally the firebricks are slightly uneven and may need a small amount of fireclay slurry just to even up a layer but on the whole you will not need anything, especially when you start laying the insulating bricks. The

Concrete blocks covered with ceramic paper.

advantages of not using any mortar are that should you wish to move or change the design of your kiln, dismantling and rebuilding ought to be comparatively easy. It is also quicker and easier to dry-lay the bricks, especially the insulating bricks, and there is a cost saving!

Refractory concrete Although I have not used any castables in the kilns described in this book refractory concrete can be useful for casting various parts of a kiln that might otherwise prove difficult, such as the skewbacks or the key blocks for the arch.

Ceramic fibre This comes in a variety of forms such as blanket, paper, board, blocks and loose fibre and is an amazing material. Its insulating qualities are remarkable and it has proved itself a valuable material for the kiln builder. It does have a negative aspect in that minute fibres can become airborne when it is used or disturbed, especially after firing. These fibres have been linked with potential long-term health worries as a possible carcinogenic. New fibres have now been developed which claim to minimise this health concern but I would still recommend the use of a suitable respirator and clothing when cutting or using any ceramic fibre materials.

The blanket is normally sold in rolls of different thickness, width and length and the other fibre products are also supplied in different formats with different working temperatures and insulation qualities. Check with your supplier that you have the best product for your intended use.

Kiln wrapped in ceramic fibre and then tin foil.

Other insulating materials

There are various other materials that can be used as back-up insulation for kilns:

- Aluminium foil (tin foil) is a wonderful final outer layer that cuts out almost all the radiant heat from the kiln and is also good for sealing in fibres from the ceramic fibre or mineral wool.
- 'Rockwool', a spun mineral wool that looks like fibreglass, can be purchased from your local builders merchant and is available in rolls, as used for loft insulation. It is excellent as a back-up insulation over the arch and can withstand a temperature of 700°C (1292°F) so

is a better material than fibreglass, whose surface can melt where it touches the kiln. Rockwool also produces 120 × 60 × 7.5cm (48 × 23½ × 29½in.) foil-backed cavity batts, that can be used to insulate the walls of the kiln.

Perforated shelves These are kiln shelves with holes, approximately 3cm (1¼in.) diameter, that I use in the fireboxes of wood-fired kilns to allow air to be introduced under the embers. You can purchase these from Acme Batt Co. or make your own with fireclay. Steve Mills, a friend and another keen kiln builder, recommends the use of the Ibstock Brick Company 'Gloucester Gold' brick (see p.27) which is produced with three holes, for making the floor of the firebox, instead of the perforated shelves, as the bricks are much more robust and cheap to replace should you need to.

Firebars These are only necessary if you intend to use wood in the firing. Some potters use metal pipe or bars but these disintegrate fairly quickly at stoneware temperatures. I always use ceramic tubular props as, with careful stoking, they will last many firings. For my large wood-fired kiln I use thick walled 7.5cm (3in.) diameter props, also purchased from Acme Batt Co.

Fitting ceramic firebars. Note how they protrude outside the kiln for removal and replacement should one get broken.

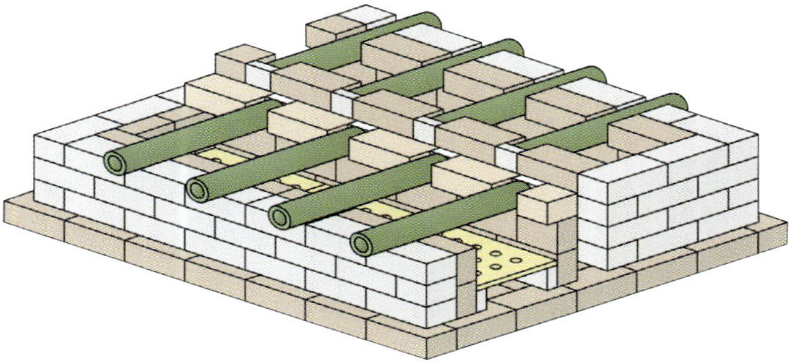

Firebars, marked green, being built into the fireboxes.

Ironwork Kiln ironwork is a necessity to support the structure, especially a sprung arch kiln that has its thrust outwards (see p.42–3).

A catenary arch kiln needs little or no ironwork as the balance of stress makes it self supporting, with all the thrust being downwards into the base of the kiln.

Other ironwork that will be needed are the corner supports for the chimney and firebox doors if firing with wood. Unless you have the experience and equipment for cutting and welding the ironwork it is best to employ a local blacksmith, steel fabricator or garage to make up the ironwork.

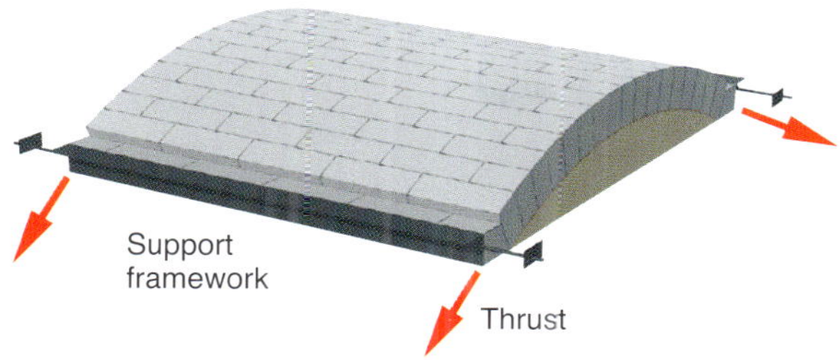

Arch showing skewback (springer) bricks and supporting ironwork.

Kiln with ironwork and 'stable doors' to firebox.

PHOTO BOB PARK.

Diagram of a kiln prop.

Kiln tubular props can be made up to any height required using combinations of prop lengths from 2.5–30cm (1–11¾in.) and extensions of 1cm–1.9cm (⅜–¾in.).

Kiln furniture A range of different size kiln props is a good investment if you want to pack your kiln to capacity. If cared for well they will endure hundreds of firings, I have props still in use that were purchased in 1973. I use the 4.5cm (1¾in.) outside diameter tubular props and fittings.

Kiln shelves, likewise, if given care and attention, should last many years and are likely to outlive your kiln!

A word of warning – if you intend to 'soda' fire, and especially if you are going to 'salt' fire, then your kiln furniture will deteriorate far quicker.

Pot with kiln prop.

Chapter 5

Kiln Design

RIGHT Joe constructing LEGO® model.
ABOVE LEGO® model – the white bricks representing firebricks and the red being the insulating bricks.

There are numerous examples of successful kilns of all different shapes and sizes. It would seem that most kiln designs will work to a greater or lesser extent as long as some basic principals of fireboxes, flues and chimney sizes are followed (details of these can be found in *The Kiln Book* by Frederick L. Olsen). However many kilns, although managing to fire to the required temperature, are inefficient, uneven and hard work to pack and fire.

When designing a new kiln I always aim to incorporate five main features:

- *Reliability* – the need for a kiln to produce good and constant results.
- *Efficiency* – able to fire using as little fuel and effort as possible.
- *Easy to use* – as comfortable and uncomplicated as possible.
- *Comfortable to pack* – packing should not be a difficult or back-breaking experience.
- *Easy to build* – no need for specialist skills or expensive tools.

When I have decided on the basic size and fuel type of kiln I am to build I find that using LEGO® to work out the brick by brick construction is very helpful. (LEGO® relates almost exactly to the scaled down dimensions of a firebrick or insulation brick.) As far as possible design your kiln to be built out of whole bricks. The fewer bricks you need to cut the quicker and easier the build will be.

For the firing chamber I aim for an approximate cube shape, this being the most efficient shape for the area enclosed when built with standard bricks and also best for circulation of heat and exchange of heat by radiation. A round or beehive shape would be more efficient but the difficulties of building and packing such a kiln far outweigh any small savings.

I mostly design down-draught kilns as I find them easier to fire evenly and less wasteful in fuel costs. Where possible, I would suggest having opposing fireboxes and positioning them under the firing chamber or within the chamber walls. External fireboxes require extra brickwork to construct and use more energy to heat up. They also radiate and lose more heat than internal fireboxes.

The three kiln designs detailed in this book have all been tried and tested and are in regular use. However, as with trying another potter's glaze recipe the results you get may not be the results you expect, and work on the glaze may be needed to acheive the effect you are looking for. Likewise with your new kiln a ceratin amount of adjustment in your firing technique may be necessary to get the best results.

Chapter 6

Tools

It is possible to build the brickwork part of a kiln with just a few basic hand tools and it should not prove difficult for someone with little or no previous experience. The photograph opposite shows the tools I used when building one of my kilns and I have listed them with their uses. The most basic and essential tools needed for building a kiln:

1. Heavy hammer and bolster, for cutting the firebricks.
2. Hand-held electric grinder with stone cutting disc, very useful but not essential for helping to cut the firebricks. (If you score the brick all the way round with the grinder, one or two hits with the hammer and bolster should cut the brick quite cleanly.)
3. Old or cheap wood saw (with large teeth) for cutting insulating bricks. You will probably need two or more saws to build the kiln, depending on how many cut bricks are needed.

TOP Scoring firebrick with angle grinder prior to breaking with bolster.

ABOVE Breaking firebrick with hammer and bolster.

LEFT Cutting an insulating brick with a saw.

The basic tools needed to build a kiln.

4 Spirit-level.
5 Large set square, also useful but not essential.
6 Tape measure long enough to measure from corner to corner of the kiln.
7 Scissors for cutting ceramic fibre also paper when designing arch former.
8 Jigsaw, for cutting wood and hardboard for arch former.
9 Dust mask or respirator, should be worn when cutting ceramic fibre and at any time when dust is being produced.
10 Sharp knife.
11 Pliers and wire cutters.
12 Screwdrivers.

Other items that may well be needed and would come in handy:

13 A drill and long masonry bit, for cutting the hole to fit the thermocouple.
14 Cutting and welding equipment, if you want to make up your own ironwork.
15 A ladder or some means of safely getting high enough to lay the arch bricks.
16 Hammer, saw, screws and nails for making the arch former.

Chapter 7

Kiln Construction

As in other parts of this book some of the information given is stating the obvious. Nevertheless, as this book is for first time kiln builders, as well as the more experienced, I feel it is best to include as much detail as possible.

Foundations Unless you are building a climbing kiln you will need a flat and stable area to build your kiln. Although a kiln with its mass of bricks and the added weight of kiln furniture and pots make up a considerable load you do not need vast foundations. A 7.5cm (3in.) thick concrete slab on a firm base is quite sufficient. If laying a new concrete base, before the concrete has set hard, it is a good idea to drill holes every 10cm (4in.) in the area the kiln is to be built on. This will allow any steam to escape should the concrete get hot. (This is not necessary if the kiln is to be built on hollow blocks.)

If you are not restricted by the height of your building I would suggest adding a layer of hollow concrete blocks on top of the concrete base. These are useful for a number of reasons: they insulate and prevent heat damage to the ground or floor under the kiln; they raise the level making packing and firing more comfortable; and they can help prevent moisture rising into the kiln if your kiln site is prone to damp.

A layer of ceramic fibre is required next, to prevent heat damaging the concrete blocks and to insulate the base of the kiln from cold air that could rise from between the hollow blocks. The fibre also helps even out any small irregularities in the block base.

Drilling holes into the concrete base having marked the area.

Firebricks on top of fibre.

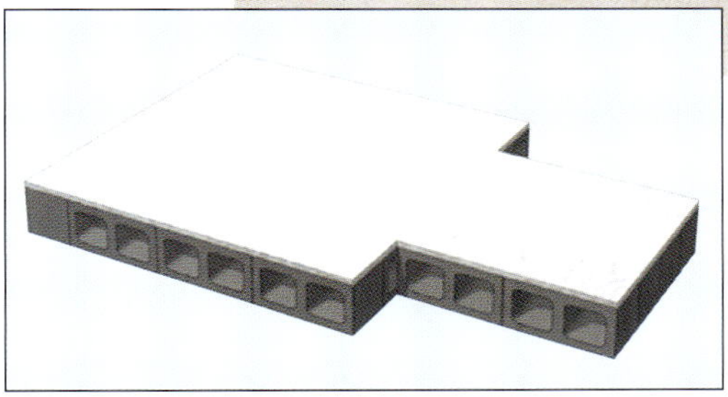

Ceramic fibre on hollow concrete blocks.

You could now start building your kiln, although I would recommend placing one complete layer of firebricks before the first of the chamber bricks are laid.

Fireboxes Kiln fireboxes are where the burning of fuel occurs and from there the heat is introduced into the kiln. As with the many diverse designs of kilns there are various different types of fireboxes. A similar firebox would be used whether you are firing with gas or oil burners but the size and shape may vary depending on the number of burners and whether they are horizontal or vertical firing. A different arrangement may be needed if you intend to fire using drip oil plate burners.

If you plan to salt glaze, you need to consider how the salt is to be introduced to the firebox. With wood firing kilns there are many choices and careful thought is required about what results you are looking for and what type of wood is available for firing. Should you require very heavy directional ashing (where flame and ash comes from one direction, so causing build up on one side of the work), or the wood you plan to use is more than 10cm (4in.) thick, then a cross-draught kiln (or Anagama-type) is advised.

For fuel efficiency and for achieving evenness of firing I have found that fireboxes situated in opposing corners with a central flue leading to the chimney are the best solution. With my wood-fired design having the fireboxes situated under the kiln chamber means less heat loss during the firing and fewer bricks used in the construction. I have used this design of kiln (see Wood-fired Kiln, pp.59–77) for the last 25 years to produce a range of domestic ware. I have also built it for a number of other potters who, I'm happy to report, find it reliable and easy to fire.

Fireboxes are best built with good quality firebricks on the inner surface as they get the full force of the flame. It is especially important if wood firing or 'salt' firing as the abrasion of the wood and the corrosive nature of the salt would soon eat away at soft insulating bricks.

Bagwalls Bagwalls are often built to protect the pots or ceramic items from the direct blast of flame from the fireboxes or to encourage the heat and flames to rise to the top of a kiln that is firing cooler in that area. You will find that the kilns that I describe and show in this book have little or no bagwalls and fire well and evenly.

Chamber walls It has been the general practice for many years to build kilns with a double skin brick wall for the chamber walls and the arch. This double wall is sometimes made up with the inner layer being firebricks and the outer insulation bricks. Other arrangements are two layers of firebrick or a high temperature insulating brick on the inside with a low temperature insulating brick on the outside. All the kilns I build and the ones detailed later have a single (11.4cm/4½in.) brick wall backed up with a layer of ceramic fibre or other material. This method I have found to be safe and efficient, also easier, cheaper and quicker to build.

Remember that although firebricks may be cheaper to buy they will work out more costly in fuel used and time spent firing, compared to a kiln built using insulating bricks. Once above the firebox height I would build the chamber walls with insulating bricks. These, if new, will require no mortar.

Arch The two main types of arch built for square or rectangular kilns are 'catenary' or 'sprung'.

The catenary arch (see below left) is favoured by some as it requires little or no supporting ironwork, the shape being self-supporting with the thrust being downwards. Its drawback is that it can make the packing of the kiln difficult as the width of the chamber narrows towards the top.

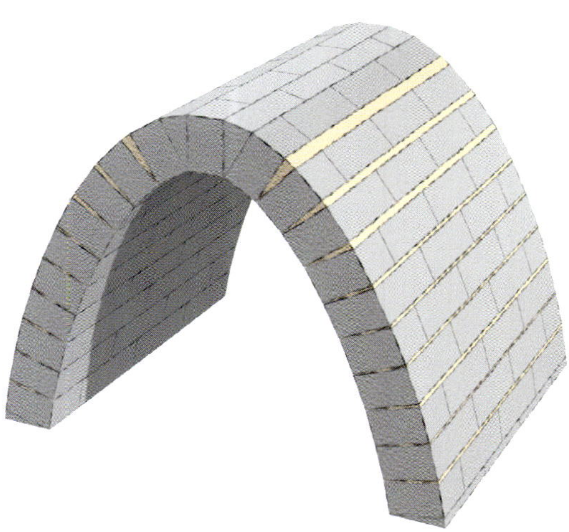

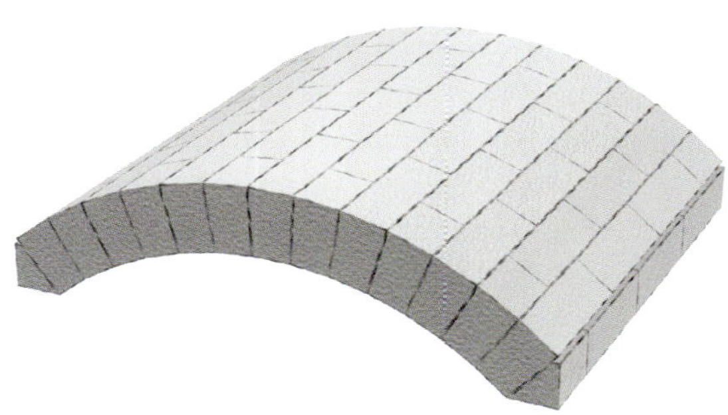

ABOVE Diagram of sprung arch.
LEFT Diagram of catenary arch.

The sprung arch kiln is the type I favour allowing an approximate cube of packing area, which should prove efficient for space and evenness of temperature.

Castable refractory concrete can be used to construct the arch but I prefer the arch built with arch bricks as once again it gives the option of dismantling and rebuilding should you wish to do so in the future.

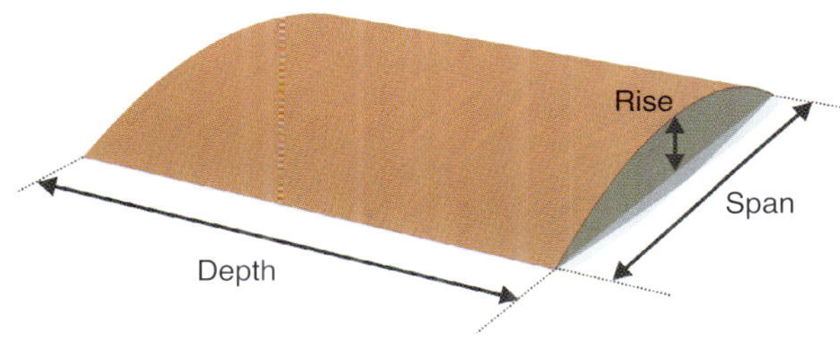

Span, rise and depth.

Constructing an arch is a straightforward process that should not prove difficult even if you have not attempted building one before. Once you have decided on the size of your kiln chamber the inside measurements will be the 'span' and the 'depth' of your arch. The other dimension required is the 'rise' of the arch. This is not critical and I usually suggest a rise of approximately 5cm per 30cm of span (2in. per 12in.).

The higher the rise of an arch the stronger it is but with good supporting ironwork any arch with a rise of a minimum of 7.5cm (3in.) will be satisfactory.

As I have already stated I recommend building your arch with side arch insulating bricks. These are fairly easy to cut from a straight 23 × 11.5 × 7.6cm (9 × 4½ × 3in.) brick. However I would advise that you get the brick supplier to cut them for you. They charge extra for this service but the bricks are all perfectly cut and it saves a lot of time and effort. You should only need to tell your supplier the span, rise and depth of the arch for them to work out how many bricks the arch will need.

Once you have the bricks you need to make an arch-former. To do this you will need some hardboard, planks of wood, some lengths of 5 × 2.5cm (2in. × 1in.) batten, a large piece of paper (big enough to more than cover the span and rise measurements), pen or pencil, scissors, jigsaw, screwdriver, screws and a flat area of floor to work on.

First lay your paper on the ground (a length of wallpaper or some newspaper stuck together will work), mark the span of the arch and then place the arch bricks on their end, tight up against each other, working from one end of your marked span to the other. You will probably have to repeat this a number of times, changing the angle of the bricks until the bricks meet the two marked points. If you find that it is impossible for the bricks to meet

Cutting the marked paper that has been folded in half.

Arch bricks around the paper template.

BELOW 1–6, Making the arch former, and placing the arch bricks.

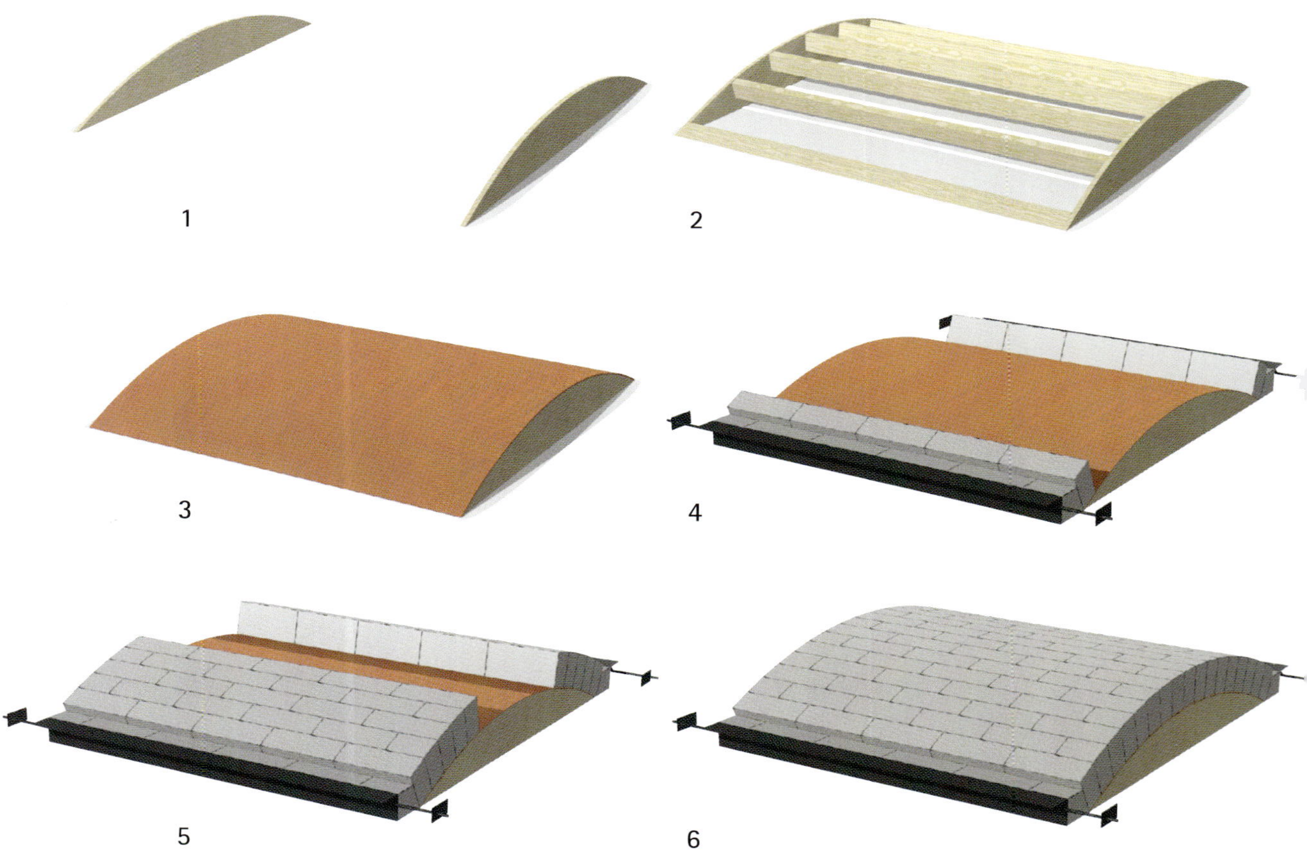

the points, either they fall short or overshoot, you can adjust the arch by adding 'straight' bricks 23 × 11.5 × 7.6cm (9 × 4.5 × 3in.) into the arch. When you have the bricks meeting the two points mark the paper on the inside of the arch. Remove the bricks, then, folding the paper in half, cut along the line. (If the mark on the paper varies from one side of the folded paper to the other, cut an average line.)

Open the paper up and lay it down on the flat ground. Now try placing the arch bricks following the shape of the cut paper. If you have the paper cut correctly, the bricks should keep to the template and the span be the right size.

Using your paper template cut two 'D' shaped pieces of wood (if the planks you have are not wide enough join two or more together). Cut the points off the ends of each of the 'D's to compensate for the thickness of the hardboard (approximately 3mm).

Cut the lengths of 5 × 2.5cm (2 × 1in.) batten, you will need seven or more depending on the size of the arch, the length being the depth of the arch minus the thickness of the two pieces of 'D' shaped boards, minus a further 5–10mm ($\frac{3}{16}$–$\frac{3}{8}$in.) so that the arch-former can be removed once the arch is built.

Screw the battens to the boards. Cut and screw the hardboard to the frame you have just constructed making sure that you keep it square.

You should now have your completed arch-former ready for building the arch. Before positioning it there is one last preparation to be completed and that is to cut the skewbacks or springer bricks. These are the wedge shaped bricks that lie on the top of the two sides of the chamber from which the arch springs. To make these you need to lay the arch-former on its side and once again place the arch bricks tightly together around the former. The gap at each end between the side of the first arch brick and line drawn out from the flat base of the 'D' is the cross section of the skewback bricks you need to cut. Mark some 'straight' bricks and cut them with a saw (if you are using insulating bricks).

When the walls of the chamber are at the correct height place the skewback bricks on the two sides. If you haven't already fitted the supporting ironwork it would be best to do so at this stage.

Support the arch-former on four lengths of 7.5 × 10cm (3 × 2in.) wood, angled from the floor of the chamber to each corner of the kiln.

Once it is level and is equally spaced each side, start placing the arch bricks starting from each side and working towards the middle. Continue to stagger the joints by starting with a half brick on one end followed with a whole brick on

Cutting a skewback brick.

Support wood for the arch former.

Arch former in place with arch bricks.

the next layer. The last central row of bricks should just fit in. If they are a bit loose don't worry, as you gently lower the arch-former by slightly moving each of the wood supports in turn towards the middle of the chamber floor, the arch bricks should lock together. DO NOT attempt to lower or remove the arch-former before you have the supporting ironwork in place. This is most important because without the ironwork the side walls will push out and the arch will almost certainly collapse.

Should you find that the last layer of arch bricks will not fit into the remaining space, you can either remove the arch bricks and lay some cardboard or blanket over the arch-former to raise the profile and then replace the arch bricks, or cut the key bricks down until they make a tight fit.

Supporting metalwork The supporting ironwork is a vital part of a sprung arch kiln. It is fairly basic and straightforward to have made and fit. It comprises of four upright lengths of angle-iron to fit to the corners of the kiln, two thrust bars that can be made from angle-iron or channel-iron, which will support the walls from the outward pressure of the arch and the tie bars and fittings to fix it all together.

Some people weld the connecting tie bars to the angle-iron, although I prefer to have the ironwork constructed so that it can be tightened, loosened or, if needed, removed, as you may want to move or rebuild your kiln some time in the future. To achieve this, short metal bars, approximately 10cm x 2.5cm (4 x 1in.) are welded to

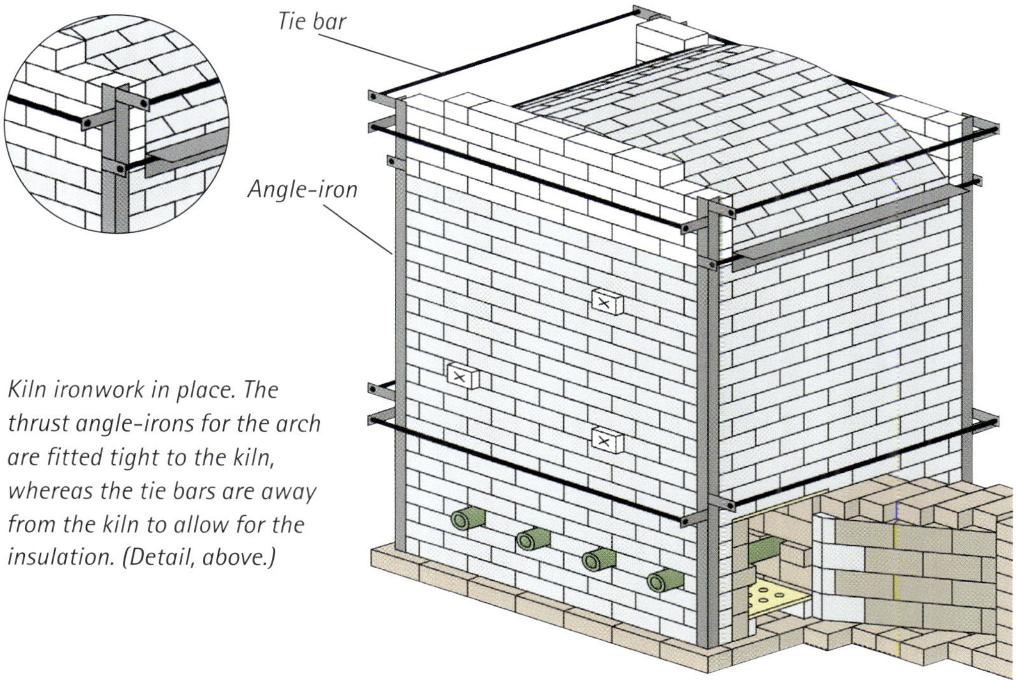

Kiln ironwork in place. The thrust angle-irons for the arch are fitted tight to the kiln, whereas the tie bars are away from the kiln to allow for the insulation. (Detail, above.)

the four upright corner angle-irons. Each has a hole cut in it, the diameter being a little larger than the tie bars to be used, and the hole being about 7.5cm (3in.) from the kiln wall (the purpose for the 7.5cm gap between the tie bar and kiln wall is to allow insulation to be fitted against the kiln). Each corner angle-iron should have four of these metal bars welded to it making sure that the tie bar, when fitted, does not obstruct a flue, firebox or wicket of the kiln (see diagram). The tie bars need not be thick in diameter, between 0.5cm and 1cm ($^{3}/_{16}$ and $^{3}/_{8}$in.) is sufficient. The ends of the tie bars need to be threaded so that with washers and nuts they can be tightened to pull the corner angle-irons firmly in place.

The two thrust bars, which are made from 7.5cm angle-iron or channel-iron, are a crucial part of the kiln. They need to fit tight against the wall of the kiln just at the point where the skewback bricks are placed and the arch started. Without their support the arch would collapse when the arch former was removed. The angle or channel-iron used needs to have some 1.5cm ($^{5}/_{8}$in.) round bar welded to each end and protruding sufficiently that it can locate into the short holed bar or piece of pipe fixed to the four corner angle-irons. This 1.5cm bar does not need to be threaded as the tie bars will keep it in place.

Similar corner angle-irons will be needed to help support the chimney if it is to be built with bricks although the tie bars for it do not need to be away from the chimney wall.

Insulation Adding insulation to anything will save some heat escaping whether it is your house, your hot water cylinder or your kiln. The more you insulate the greater the savings of heat, so reducing fuel consumption, which will lead to an economy of costs. Even with an efficient gas, oil or wood-fired kiln approximately 40% of the heat introduced disappears up the chimney. A badly insulated kiln, combined with the heat loss via the chimney, could result in a slow or no rise at high temperature. Remember that to achieve an increase in temperature in the kiln depends on the heat that is generated in the fireboxes being greater than the heat stored or lost.

If you build a kiln as I suggest with the chamber walls only one brick thickness, even though these may be high quality insulation bricks, you will require further backup insulation. One layer of 2.5cm (1in.) ceramic blanket on the outside of a kiln could result in up to 20% savings in fuel costs, especially if you intend firing to stoneware temperatures. A 5cm (2in.) ceramic blanket or further insulation will increase the saving and is extra beneficial if you are firing with wood. Constant attention to the kiln can be tiring enough without the added ingredient of heat exhaustion from working close to a kiln that is radiating a lot of heat.

There are various other alternative materials that can be used as backup insulation. One that I regularly use is a mineral wool called 'Rockwool', a product used in house construction for insulation purposes and is similar to fibreglass but has the advantage of not melting at red heat. The final layer of insulation I like to add to a kiln is aluminium foil (tin foil). This is cheap but very effective for cutting down radiated heat and is also beneficial by sealing in the fibres from the other insulation. To hold the foil in place some wire mesh is effective.

Flues The flues of a kiln are the passages where the flames, fumes and heat travel through to exit by the chimney.

The internal flues, as the name suggests, are the ones within the kiln and in the case of a down-draught kiln are under the main chamber. These will be subject to high temperatures and should be constructed using good refractory bricks. As they are also usually part of the floor structure and will be supporting the weight of the pots and kiln shelves when packed, I always build these with firebricks. The external flue is the connecting channel between the chamber and the chimney. This will experience lower temperatures and does not have to support anything except itself so can be built with whatever refractories you still have.

Chimney The chimney of any 'flame' kiln is necessary to expel the fumes away from the kiln area. This is vitally important, especially if the kiln is in a building or confined space, because one of the gases produced, as a waste product if you are firing with a reduction atmosphere, is carbon monoxide, a deadly gas that is invisible and odourless.

Propane (LPG) gas kilns require the smallest chimney as the pressure from the bottled gas sucks air in around the burner and so reduces the need for a large chimney to create the draught. If you have forced air propane burners the kiln only requires a vent capable of expelling the fumes. Natural gas and oil both require more of a chimney but the

Internal central flue and exit flue to chimney.

largest chimney (if comparing kilns fired with different fuels but of the same chamber capacity) would be the wood-fired kiln as it relies solely on the draught produced by the chimney to suck the air in needed to combust the burning wood.

The height and dimensions of the chimney will depend on the size of your kiln. Other factors affecting how tall it needs to be are the height of the surrounding buildings (as they can cause down-draughts), the altitude at which the kiln is built and the distance the chimney is from the kiln. (Michael Cardew, in his book *Pioneer Pottery*, states that you need an extra 1.2m/4ft of vertical chimney for each 0.3m/1ft of horizontal flue.)

With all kiln chimneys it is better to err on the side of caution by making them too large, because the pull to the chimney can always be reduced during a firing by sliding a damper in or taking some bricks out of the chimney. When building the chimney, remember to build in a slide damper and to leave some loose bricks near the base which can be removed (as a passive damper) if necessary.

Chapter 8

Preparing the Kiln for Packing and Firing

Before you pack your kiln, especially if it is a first firing with new kiln shelves and props, there are a number of checks and some preparations that need to be attended to.

- Look over the inside of the kiln and down into the fireboxes and flues to make sure nothing has been left, or fallen, where it should not be.

- If it is a new kiln you should brush over the inside of the chamber with a soft brush or even vacuum clean the bricks, because there will be dust and loose bits of brickwork produced in the construction, just waiting to fall and stick to your favourite pot. It is worth spending a couple of minutes brushing the inside of the kiln on subsequent firings to ensure you don't suffer from this problem.

- Some potters like to coat the inside of a new kiln with a refractory wash, either a proprietary mix from a ceramic supplier or made by themselves. Personally I prefer not to cover the inside of the kiln as I have found that all the mixes I have tried in the past eventually start to fracture from the brickwork and bits begin to flake off.

- If the thermocouple is to be fitted through the top of the kiln it could be done now, as long as it is not in danger of being knocked during packing. If fitted later do remember that it could push some dirt through onto pots below so care should be taken when installing it. To fit a thermocouple probe through a kiln wall or arch is a simple process, as long as the brick it is to go through is an insulating brick. A drill with a masonry bit, of the correct diameter, that is long enough to protrude through the brickwork, will easily drill through. The thermocouple can then be carefully pushed through, but do take care as they are fragile. The probe only needs to have about 2.5cm (1in.) of its tip through into the kiln. Pack some ceramic fibre around the thermocouple where it exits the kiln to prevent the outer end getting too hot.

- Kiln shelves and props will also need attention especially if you are firing to stoneware temperatures. They are costly items but if looked after properly can give hundreds of firings. A thin refractory wash on the ends of the props and top surface of the kiln shelf will help prevent anything sticking.

  An alternative method is to use dry calcined alumina, which is like very fine, free running sand or table salt in texture. Props can be coated by dabbing each end onto a wet sponge and then into a container of calcined alumina. The shelves require a dusting over the top surface but care must be taken not to allow any to fall off the shelves onto the pots below. If using this method when you come to unpack the kiln brush the loose alumina into a container to be reused next firing. If you are wood firing pour the collected alumina through a 40 grade mesh sieve to remove any gritty ash deposits.

If anything has stuck to a shelf from a previous firing a hand-held grinder with a stone blade will clean it off but do be careful not to damage the shelf or yourself! Always wear protective goggles. A safer method, but harder work, would be to rub down the shelf with a hand-held silicon carbide or carborundum stone.

- Before placing a shelf in the kiln always brush the sides and base to remove anything loose. Props should be checked to make sure they are clean, fitting together evenly and are all the same size for the layer you are about to pack.

- Always prop on three points per shelf, four propping points is not necessary and will only make the shelf rock and could cause the shelf to crack.

  Load the kiln as normal, I won't go into details of how to pack as this is covered by other books, suffice to say that you should make sure that no glaze surface is touching a shelf, prop or other pot.

- Check that you have plenty of fuel and some to spare – what you don't use will not be wasted as it will be needed for the next firing. The worst scenario, having spent many hours firing, is to run out of fuel just before you reach temperature. In the case of wood firing not only do you need an abundance of wood but it must be seasoned and thoroughly dry.

I have a personal experience of the importance of this: One winter, while potting in the West Highlands of Scotland, the weather had been especially wet. Although I had stored the kiln wood under cover for three months and thought it was dry enough, there was still moisture in it because of the humidity. The firing went well up to about 1100°C (2012°F) but then the rise in temperature started to slow. By the time the kiln reached 1200°C (2192°F) it was midnight and the time I would normally expect the firing to be ending. With another 100°C (212°F) to go the temperature refused to budge. Luckily I had some friends helping me but by then we had been stoking for twenty hours and were getting weary. Five hours later, after trying everything, we had only managed 1225°C (2237°F), still seriously under-fired. At this point I was calling for help from Saint Jude, the patron saint of lost causes. Anyway, Saint Jude didn't turn up but my neighbour, having woken at 5am to see all our lights on, came to find out if there was anything wrong. Having recounted our tale of woe, she astounded me by saying that in her out-buildings she had plenty of dry wood, her winter supply, and we were to help ourselves. We, and the kiln reacted immediately and in under an hour 1300°C (2372°F) had been reached and the firing saved!

Chapter 9

Temperature Measurement

The temperature within the kiln can be measured and monitored in various ways. By looking through one of the spy holes the colour inside the kiln will give an indication of its temperature to an experienced eye but the use of a pyrometer and thermocouple removes the guesswork and is generally used.

Colour of temperature	°C	°F
Lowest visible dull red in dark conditions	470	878
Lowest visible dull red in daylight	550 - 650	1022 - 1202
Dark red to cherry red	650 - 750	1202 - 1382
Cherry red to bright cherry red	750 - 815	1382 - 1499
Bright cherry red to orange	815 - 900	1499 - 1652
Orange to yellow	900 - 1090	1652 - 1994
Yellow to bright, light yellow	1090 - 1315	1994 - 2399
Bright, light yellow to white	1315 - 1500	2399 - 2732

The digital pyrometer is an excellent aid to firing as it gives an immediate response of any increase, or decrease, of temperature but it can be inaccurate especially at high temperatures. Furthermore, a pyrometer may fail during a firing. For this reason I would always recommend the use of pyrometric cones in conjunction with the pyrometer.

Pyrometric cones, which are made from a carefully calculated mixture of ceramic materials are designed to bend at a given temperature. They are all marked with a number that relates to their bending temperatures. However, they do not really measure temperatures but rather heatwork or the combined effect of heat and time. Glazes also react in the

Orton cones 9,10 and 11.

Cone number	Squatting temperature when heated at: 60°C per hour	108°F per hour	150°C per hour	270°F per hour
09	915	1679	923	1693
08	945	1733	955	1751
07	973	1783	984	1803
06	991	1816	999	1830
05	1031	1888	1046	1915
04	1050	1922	1060	1940
03	1086	1987	1101	2014
02	1101	2014	1120	2048
01	1117	2043	1137	2079
1	1136	2077	1154	2109
2	1142	2088	1162	2124
3	1152	2106	1168	2134
4	1168	2134	1186	2167
5	1177	2151	1196	2185
6	1201	2194	1222	2232
7	1215	2219	1240	2264
8	1236	2257	1263	2305
9	1260	2300	1280	2336
10	1285	2345	1305	2381
11	1294	2361	1315	2399
12	1306	2383	1326	2419
13	1321	2410	1346	2455

Table for large Orton pyrometric cones.

'Kiln dragons' before and after firing.

same manner to heatwork, making cones a better indicator when the firing is finished, than a temperature reading from a pyrometer.

They are normally used in sets of three. The middle cone being the correct firing temperature required, with a lower melting cone in front to indicate that the end temperature is approaching and a higher one behind to warn not to over-fire the kiln.

View through spy hole with cones beginning to bend.

A separate cone is often used and placed nearer the spy hole if you are going to have a reduction firing. This cone would bend between 950°C (1742°F) and 1000°C (1832°F) depending on the temperature you require to end oxidation and start reduction. However, if left in the kiln this cone would melt into a puddle of glaze at the final firing temperature and could ruin a kiln shelf. Two ways to prevent this are:

1 Taking a small lump of clay, position your cone at one end and pinch out a little reservoir in front of it that will be large enough to accommodate the cone as it melts.
2 Roll and fix a small ring to the back of clay holding the cone then, when the cone bends, use a metal rod to fish out the cone through the spy hole.

Draw rings, although not for temperature measurement, are another useful aid to firing especially if you are salt or soda firing but also for a regular glaze firing. They are clay rings, approximately 2.5cm (1in.) in diameter (depending on the size of your kiln spy holes), with a flat base, so they will stand without rolling. The top half of the ring is glazed and then placed on a shelf inside the kiln, next to a spy hole, so they can be withdrawn using a metal rod at the end of the firing to check if the glaze has melted or in the case of salt or soda, to see if a sufficient build up of glaze has occurred. The draw rings taken out of the kiln at top temperature will not give much indication of the finished colour of the fired clay or glaze when it has cooled – they are only useful to let you know that the glaze has melted. For this reason it is always best to glaze the rings in the glaze that has the highest maturing temperature.

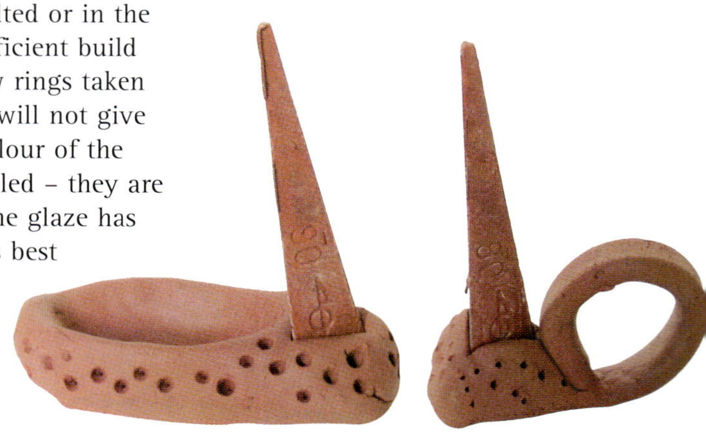

Reduction cones.

Chapter 10

Kiln Firing

The kiln is packed, the wicket (door of the kiln) is bricked up, the chimney damper is open, you have more than enough fuel but before you fire I would suggest two other considerations: get a weather report, if you are in for a storm or high winds it may be best to delay for more favourable conditions; and organise some assistance especially if you are wood firing.

Keep a detailed kiln log of each firing with not only time and temperature readings but also weather conditions, wind strength and direction, air temperature and even barometric pressure as all these things can have an effect on a firing.

Also, log all alterations you make, whether it is turning the burners up or down, how you stoke, if you have made changes to the primary or secondary air or adjusted the dampers. A properly kept kiln log will prove a real asset for future firings as it will help you imitate a good firing and hopefully help identify where you went wrong in the case of a poor firing. A useful tip that helps with keeping your kiln logs standardized, given to me some years ago, and one I have used ever since, is to have a 'kiln clock'. All this involves is having a clock by your kiln log that you set to 12 o'clock (or 00:00 if it is digital) when you start firing. Then any reading will give you the time span you have been firing and any subsequent firing you will be able to refer back to make an easy comparison.

Keeping a kiln graph to record the temperature is a useful visual aid to firing, and proves handy for future reference. Another tip, given to me by Jonathan Chiswell Jones, a potter friend, is to mark out a 'perfect firing' graph and protect this behind clear plastic. You then mark your new graph on the plastic as you fire, keeping as close as you can to your perfect firing. If you use water based ink the plastic can be wiped clean for the next firing.

The type of firing you choose and the results you are looking for will determine whether you fire with an oxidation or reduction atmosphere in your kiln.

Ray Finch writing his kiln log.

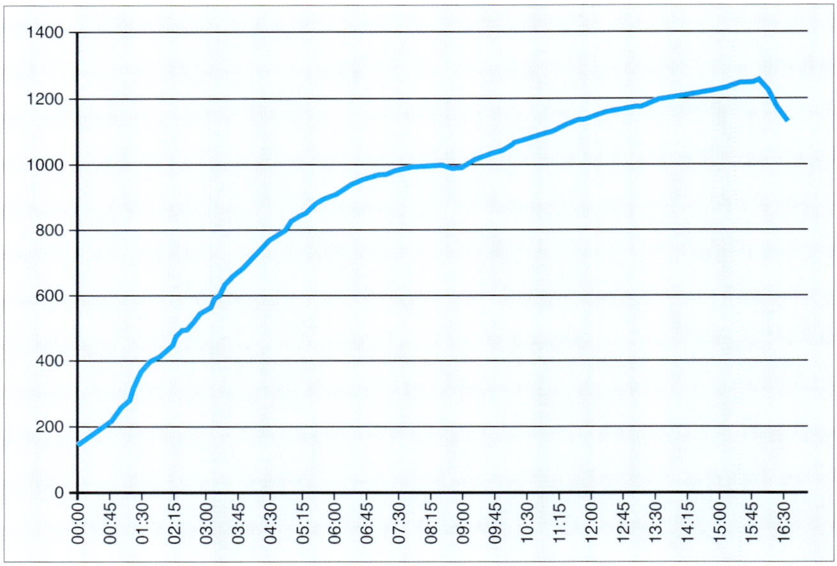

Graph showing temperature in degrees centigrade against time in hours and minutes, for one of my raw-glazed (once-fired) wood firings.

Biscuit firing is always done with an oxidising atmosphere as it is important to burn out carbon and sulphur that are present in clay. This happens between 700°C (1292°F) and 1000°C (1832°F) when the carbon and sulphur combine with the oxygen to form monoxide, dioxide and trioxide gases (CO, CO_2, SO, SO_2 and SO_3). Earthenware firings are also normally fired in an oxidising atmosphere.

In a 'flame' kiln an oxidising firing is achieved by the introduction of sufficient air to totally combust the fuel entering the kiln. This should give a clear atmosphere within the firing chamber and a total lack of visible flame at the damper or from any spy hole. Only enough air for full combustion should be allowed to enter the firebox as an excess of air can have a cooling effect that can prevent the kiln from gaining temperature. If burners are being used, the air entering the burners and mixing with the gas or oil before combustion is called 'primary air'. The air that enters through other openings in the firebox is called 'secondary air'.

Reduction is the action of taking oxygen away from the metal oxides in the clay and glaze so changing their colour, (an example of this would be copper red glazes that can only be produced in a reduction atmosphere). In a firing this is obtained by incomplete combustion of the fuel. This can be achieved by adding more fuel to the firebox or cutting down the primary or secondary air, so reducing the oxygen to the burning fuel. The draw of the chimney is usually diminished when reduction is started which will cause a back-pressure within the kiln. This can be achieved by a slide damper or by taking bricks out of the chimney, which is called a 'passive damper'. Some flame at the spy holes should be evident when reduction is taking place, although it is sometimes difficult to see, especially if firing with propane gas. A good way to test

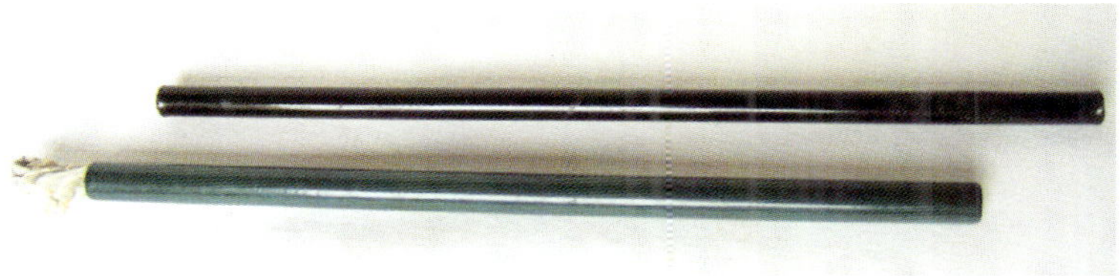

The bottom tube has the paper sticking out of the end. The top bar fits inside the tube to push the paper out ready for the next test.

for reduction when firing with gas (if you cannot afford an oxygen probe) is to take out one of the spy hole bricks and put a wooden spill into the hole. If the spill bursts into flame there is insufficient reduction within the kiln but if the spill just chars within the spy hole then reduction is being achieved. A simple tool to help with this test is a metal tube, approximately 40cm (15¾in.) long with an inner diameter of 1cm–1.5cm (⅜–⅝in.) into which you insert a twist of newspaper so it just fits inside the tube with about 2cm (¾in.) sticking out of the end. When you want to test for reduction hold the metal tube with its end just inside the spy hole, the paper sticking out of the end will only char if there is sufficient reduction. If the paper bursts into flame inside the spy hole then the atmosphere is an oxidising one.

Over-reducing does not have any benefits, it is wasteful of fuel and can cause a halt in the rise or even a loss of temperature. Over-stoking is a common mistake, whether you are firing with gas, oil or wood. If a point is reached when the temperature is sticking or you want to increase it, the natural impulse is to add more fuel. This can result in the temperature dropping – you add more fuel and it drops further! In this scenario, what is happening is that the increase of fuel is making the kiln over reduce. You need to return to an oxidation atmosphere, or if you are trying to reduce, lessening the reduction. You will achieve this by cutting back the fuel input or increasing the primary or secondary air to your fuel mix. This can be accomplished in various ways depending on how you are firing but generally by opening more air controls in the firebox or increasing the draw in the chimney (which in turn will suck in more air at the firebox).

Firing schedule

Most ceramics require a rather slow steady firing schedule, with special care during some periods.

With a bisque (biscuit) firing, although the ware will feel and appear to be dry, it will still contain some water so the firing must start on a very low flame. This period up to 100°C (212°F), known as 'candelling' or 'smoking' the kiln, should not be rushed as any moisture within the clay, if heated too fast, could turn to steam and crack or even explode the ware. It is advisable to continue with this slow rise for a further 50–100°C (122–212°F) to allow the cooler parts of the kiln to catch up and for even longer if there are large or thick pieces being fired. This drying out stage is completed when no moisture can be detected escaping from the kiln. You can check this by seeing if condensation occurs on a cold piece of glass held near the spy hole.

Joe stoking.

Once this danger point has passed, firing can proceed at a faster rate, 100–150°C (212–302°F) per hour is a reasonable rate for most pottery. However, it does depend on the size, thickness and type of clay of the ceramic pieces in the kiln.

Between 450°C (842°F) and 650°C (1202°F) the chemically combined water is driven off, changing the clay forever so that it can never again be returned to a plastic state. As long as the temperature rise is steady and does not suddenly jump then this period should not present any problems.

Organic matter in the clay burns out at between 750°C (1382°F) and 900°C (1652°F) so it is important to make sure that there is an oxidising atmosphere in the kiln during this part of the firing. Most clays would be bisque fired between 950°C (1742°F) and 1000°C (1832°F) so I would recommend slowing the firing down from 900°C (1652°F) so that the kiln can even up in temperature. Once your final temperature is reached, firing stops, the dampers are closed and the kiln clammed up and allowed to cool slowly.

If you are raw-glazing and once-firing, you would follow the above bisque firing schedule but then continue with the firing. I have found that with once-firing most clays need a temperature soak for about one hour at about 980°C (1796°F) to ensure all the organic material has burnt off.

For a glaze firing, with pots that have already been bisque fired, a faster rise of temperature can be achieved to reach 1000°C (1832°F). From that point on the speed of firing is likely to depend on whether you are firing in oxidation or reduction and how much heat can be generated in your fireboxes but it is unlikely you can damage the ware in the kiln by firing too fast from 1000°C (1832°F).

(Fred Olsen describes in *The Kiln Book* fast firing from start to 1300°C (2372°F) in under five hours, but I would not recommend you attempt such a schedule. Depending on the size of your kiln an 8–12 hour firing would be considered normal.)

Once the final temperature has been reached I would recommend holding the temperature for at least 30 minutes to let the kiln 'soak'. This will help the glaze settle and help the temperature in the kiln to even out.

When you are satisfied that the firing has finished, the burners are turned off or, in the case of wood firing, stoking stops. Some stoneware potters choose to 'crash cool', that is to leave the fireboxes open and full draw to the chimney, to about 1100°C (2012°F). The reason for doing this is that the quick cooling will reduce cristobalite forming in the fired clay. (Too much cristobalite can cause cracking when it suddenly shrinks at 226°C/439°F.) Another reason is that if you are like me and impatient to see the results the crash cool will speed up the cooling cycle by three to four hours. This should not affect any shiny glazes but if you have matt glazes that need to re-crystalline on cooling it is probably best not to crash cool and to 'clam-up' straight away. To clam-up you need to close all openings to the kiln and close off the chimney so that all the heat is sealed in and the kiln and pack cool slowly.

The final job before retiring is to clear around the kiln; make sure there is nothing that can burn or melt within a minimum of 1m (3⅓ft). Check that there are no cracks that have opened up during the firing and if there are, close them with ceramic fibre or a mix of sand and clay. Leave some ventilation open if the kiln is in a building as the heat given off is considerable. Remove anything that could be affected by excessive heat, including your digital pyrometer.

My wood-fired kiln part unpacked.

Chapter 11

Possible Problems

Unfortunately there are many dangers awaiting your ceramic masterpiece once in the kiln! I will touch on the main problems but there is detailed information in a number of books should you experience any of these difficulties.

Firing too fast At the start of the firing this can cause ware to crack or explode. Raw pots being bisque fired or once-fired are most at risk. The thicker the ware the slower this early stage must be.

Carbon trapping This occurs because the organic matter in the clay has not fully been burnt out during the 750°C (1382°F) to 900°C (1652°F) stage. To prevent this, make sure that throughout this period you have a clean oxidised atmosphere to burn up all the carbon present in the clay. If there are thick pieces of work in the kiln you may need to soak or take a couple of hours through this phase.

Bloating This is caused by gases attempting to escape after the outer surface has become impervious due to vitrification. The main culprits are carbon monoxide and dioxide still being produced from carbon not being fully burnt after the outer layer of the ware has sealed. As with carbon trapping allow enough time before 1000°C (1832°F) for all the carbon to be burnt.

Oxidation This is not a problem unless you are trying to achieve clay and glaze colours that require reduction! Reduced stoneware clays and glazes have a warmth and depth not present if oxidised. To prevent oxidation in a stoneware clay reduction must be started before the outer layer has sealed, which in most cases is between 1050°C (1922°F) and 1100°C (2012°F). I generally recommend starting reduction at 950–1000°C (1742–1832°F). Likewise, for glazes to reduce the reduction must begin before the glaze starts to melt.

Over-reduction This is not so much a danger to the ware in the kiln but a waste of fuel and likely to prolong the firing as temperature rises will be small, nonexistent or even fall if over-reduction takes place.

Dunting Appears as very fine hair cracks in bisque ware, and is caused by stresses in the cooling when cristobalite and quartz inversions suddenly decrease in volume. It usually happens in soft fired bisque pots that have been cooled too quickly through the

573°C (1063°F) and 226°C (439°F) stages. It is often quite difficult to see these cracks but they generally show up when you glaze the ware. Although only very fine cracks at the bisque phase, they unfortunately tend to open up during the glaze firing. To remedy this problem, should it occur, fire your bisque higher – 950°C to 1000°C (1742 to 1922°F) and make sure the kiln cools slowly by keeping all the dampers and spy holes closed until you reach 200°C (392°F). Another way of preventing dunting is to raw glaze and once-fire, that way the ware has its full strength and can withstand the cooling stresses.

Under-firing Opening a kiln to find you have under-fired is a frustrating experience, especially after all the time, effort and expense and knowing just another half an hour and few degrees more would have given a perfect result. This is a common fault with a new kiln, especially if you are firing new untried glazes. The best way to avoid under-firing is to place pyrometric cones and fire until the correct one has bent over.

Over-firing This is equally maddening but more serious than under-firing because you cannot make the ware better by re-firing to the correct temperature. Just 10°C (50°F) above the required temperature may cause little or no problems but 20°C (68°F) could mean glazes running and sticking to shelves and pots deforming and blistering. Further increases would result in more deterioration. Over-firing can also damage the kiln, shelves and props. Again, a close eye on the cones towards the end of the firing should prevent this.

Shattering and crazing These problems can be aggravated by cooling too quickly. However if your work suffers from either of these it would be best to make changes to the clay body or glaze to alleviate the troubles.

Three jugs by Joe Finch.

The pots from one of Joe Finch's firings in his wood-fired kiln.

The Kilns

Wood-fired Kiln

'The wood-fired kiln, built in 1997 by Joe Finch for the Crafts Council of Ireland's Pottery Skills Course, has proved to be a great asset to the course's facilities. The kiln was easy and quick to build but most importantly produced great pots from the first firing on.

From the point of view of running a training course however the beauty of this kiln lies in it's ability to fire quickly and evenly making it an ideal kiln for anyone wood firing for the first time.

The kiln has given many students their first taste of wood firing and an introduction to wood-fired aesthetics. They only have to fire the kiln once to gain the confidence to fire it a second time with little supervision needed.'

Gus Mabelson

'My wood kiln and I are very happy together. Joe designed and built it about seven years ago and for the past three years I've been mainly firing it alone.

I fire about once every three months and use short pine pointings for fuel (the waste wedgy bits left over from making fence stakes). This works well, the wood is very local, cheap and doesn't involve sawing at all. I stack it for a few months prior to use. The disadvantages being a greater strain on my arms when loading and increased heat stress, as I need to be closer to the fireboxes, when stoking. However, the kiln thrives on it and generally goes up smoothly, depending on weather conditions. It is situated under an open roof in a windy valley. As I make quite large sculptural pieces I load the work one day and fire the next, beginning early and keep it going to about 1300°C (2372°F), introducing soda painted onto the fuel. When I'm too hot and tired I stop, usually after about 15 hours. Because of the system of secondary burning, I never have to rake out piles of ashes and nothing is wasted. I have only changed the fire bars once during this time and it was easy just slipping the new kiln props into place.

Alternative uses for the kiln have been discovered including; a hide for watching wildlife and ricotta cheese making on the flue during cooling.'

Meri Wells

'In 2000 Joe Finch built a 45cu. ft/1.27sq. m (packing space) modified quick fire kiln at my pottery in Greystoke, Cumbria. I have fired it, by myself, almost every month since then. The firing takes between 10–11 hours to cone 9 and uses about 2cu. m (2.6cu. yd) of wood. It has been the easiest and most efficient wood kiln I have ever fired.'

Bob Park

The kiln diagrams and photographs shown here are for a kiln designed for right-handed stokers. If you require a kiln suitable for left-handed stokers you need to construct a mirror image of this kiln.

NB: The photographs show a kiln built onto a concrete base, whereas the diagrams show an alternative method of building onto concrete blocks.

PHOTOGRAPHS BY BOB PARK.

Prepare a flat level base large enough for the kiln and chimney.

1 Measuring kiln dimensions onto concrete slab that has been drilled with holes to let any steam that may be produced escape. LEGO® model in foreground.

2 Dry placing the firebricks onto the concrete slab.

Concrete blocks with firebricks covering the kiln base, all these to be placed without mortar. A layer of ceramic fibre could be laid under the firebricks for extra insulation.

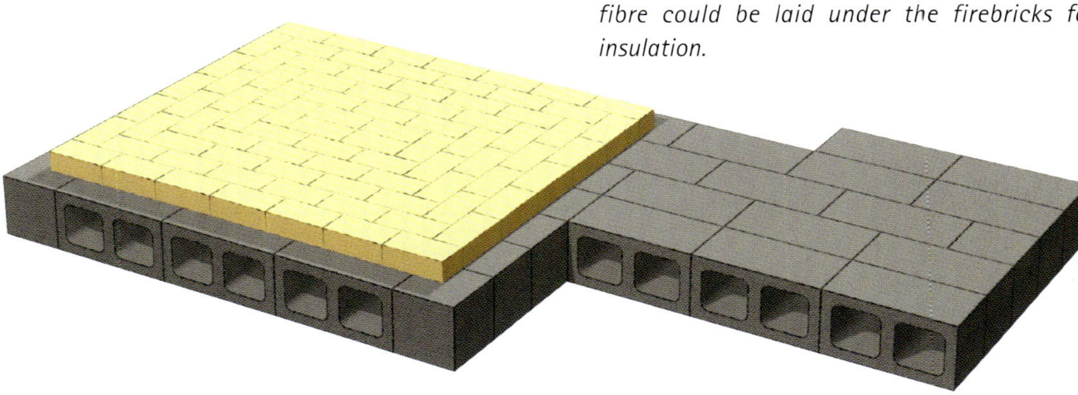

3 Squaring up the first layer of insulating bricks, some of these will be removed for the firebox and exit flues.

4 Fireboxes and central flue being formed with firebricks. The perforated shelves being used to check the width of the fireboxes.

5 Forming the base of the fireboxes and checking the perforated shelves fit onto the cut insulating brick supports.

BELOW *Forming the fireboxes and central flue. The outer insulating bricks (grey/white) are laid flat, inside these are firebricks (yellow) placed on their edge, with cut insulating bricks 3.7 × 7.5 × 23cm (1.5 × 3 × 9in.) to support the perforated shelves.*

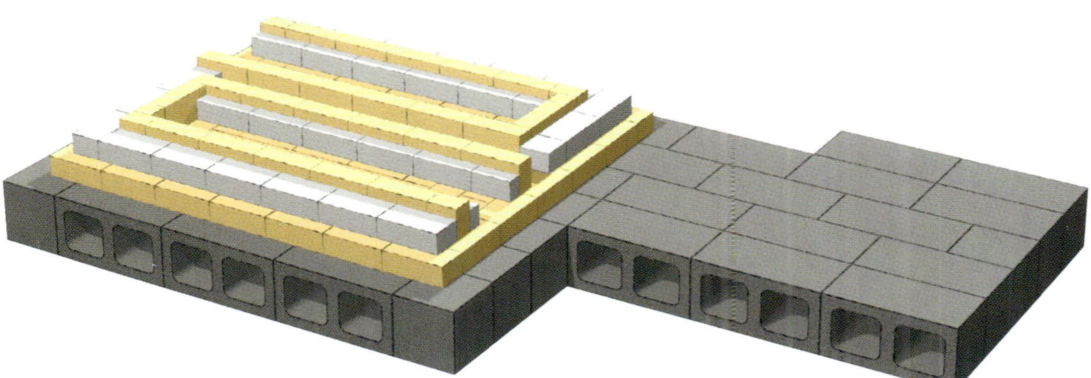

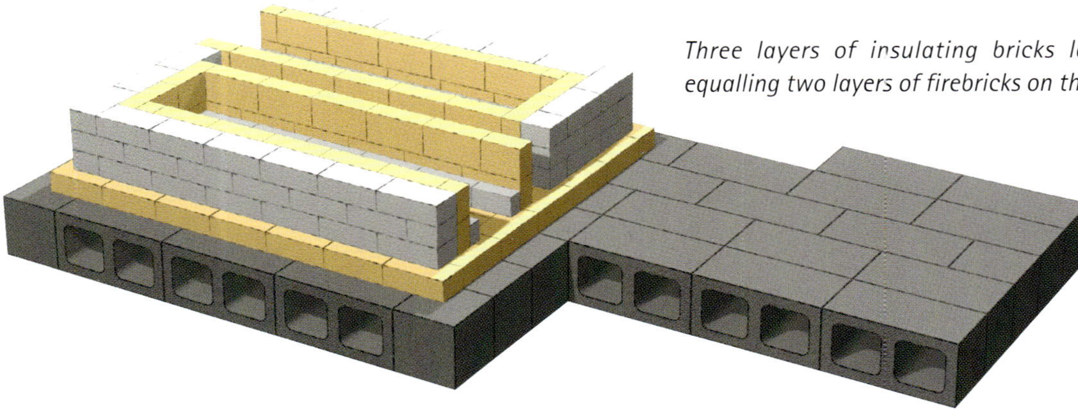

Three layers of insulating bricks laid flat equalling two layers of firebricks on their side.

6 Three layers of insulating bricks dry laid with firebricks fixed with fireclay slurry.

7 Fitting the 7.5cm (3in.) diameter ceramic props as firebars on the first firebox.

8 Fitting last of the firebars.

9 Both sets of firebars in position, with firebox walls continuing and flue and chimney base being placed.

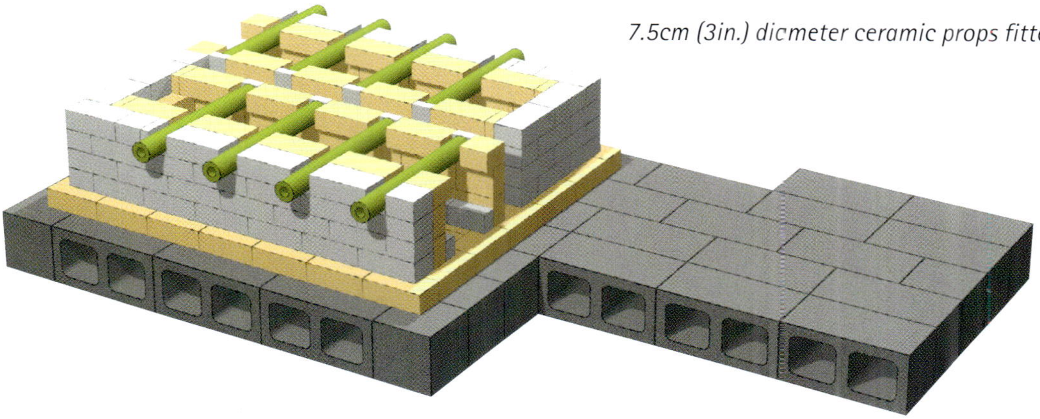

7.5cm (3in.) diameter ceramic props fitted as firebars.

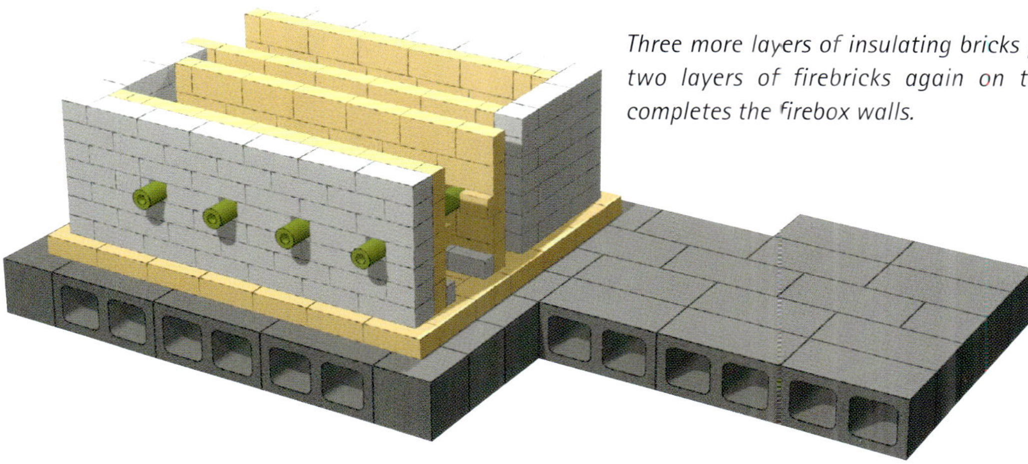

Three more layers of insulating bricks placed flat with two layers of firebricks again on their edge. This completes the firebox walls.

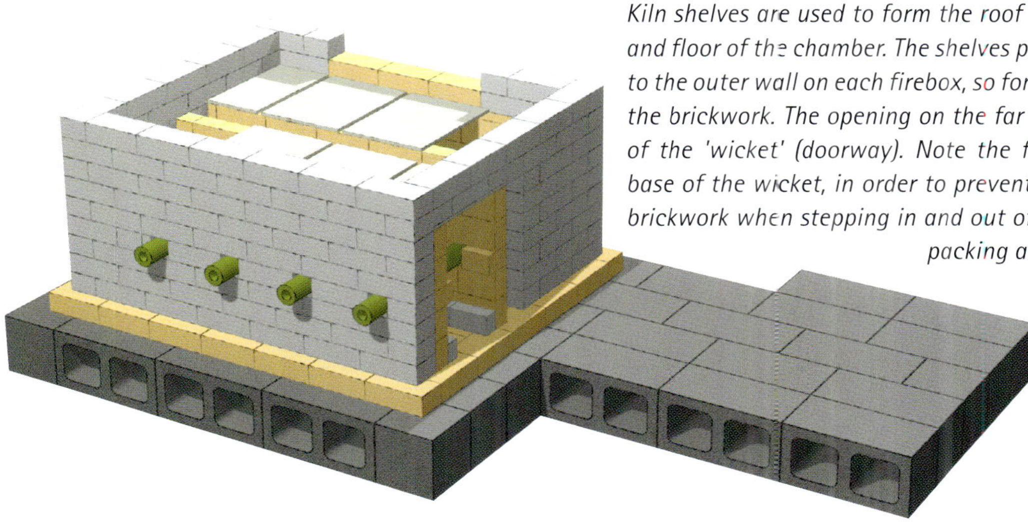

Kiln shelves are used to form the roof of the fireboxes and floor of the chamber. The shelves protrude through to the outer wall on each firebox, so forming a lintel for the brickwork. The opening on the far side is the start of the 'wicket' (doorway). Note the firebricks at the base of the wicket, in order to prevent damage to the brickwork when stepping in and out of the kiln during packing and unloading.

10 Fireboxes completed and first full layer of the kiln chamber in place.

11 Chamber walls continue above the fireboxes.

Chamber walls continue.

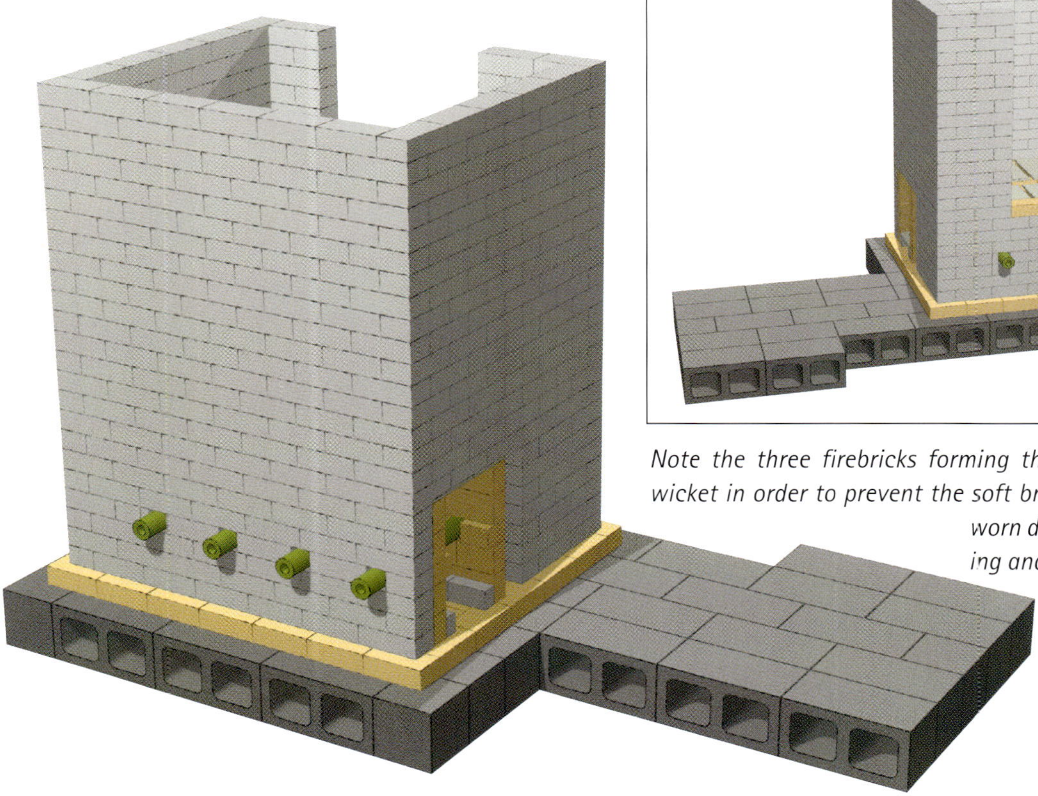

Note the three firebricks forming the bottom of the wicket in order to prevent the soft bricks from getting worn down during packing and unloading.

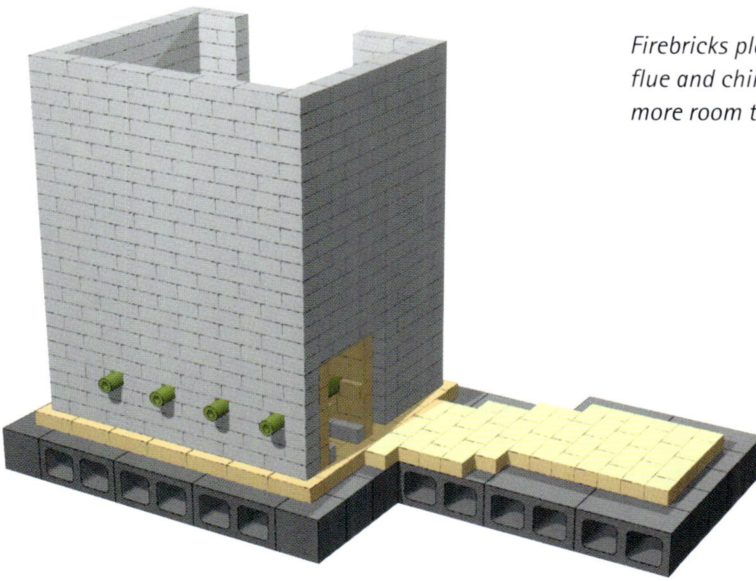

Firebricks placed on concrete blocks for the base of the flue and chimney. Note the brickwork is offset allowing more room to stoke the firebox on that side.

RIGHT *Chimney is started leaving gap for flue.*

Connecting flue to the chimney. Note the use of insulating bricks where awkward cut bricks are needed.

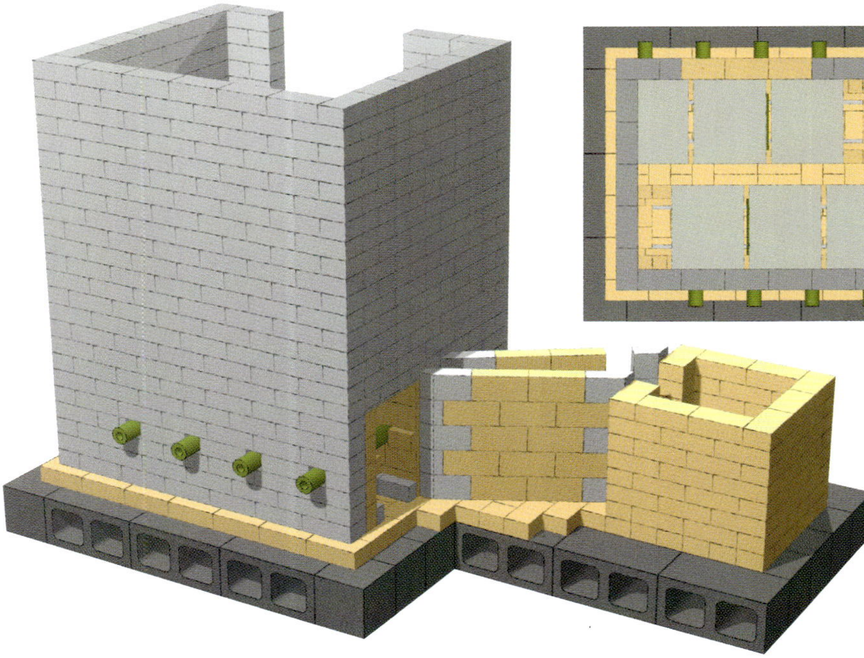

(a)

Flue to chimney completed, except for the top closing shelves. Note the 12cm (4¾in.) gap in the flue for placing loose bricks that can be used as passive dampers and also for sliding in a kiln shelf to close off the kiln at the end of the firing.

(a) *Plan of aiagram shown above.* (b) *Detail of flue and start of chimney.*

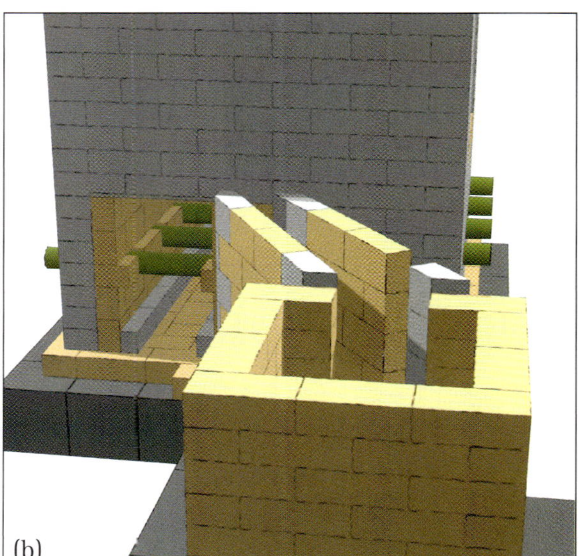

(b)

12 View from chimney side.

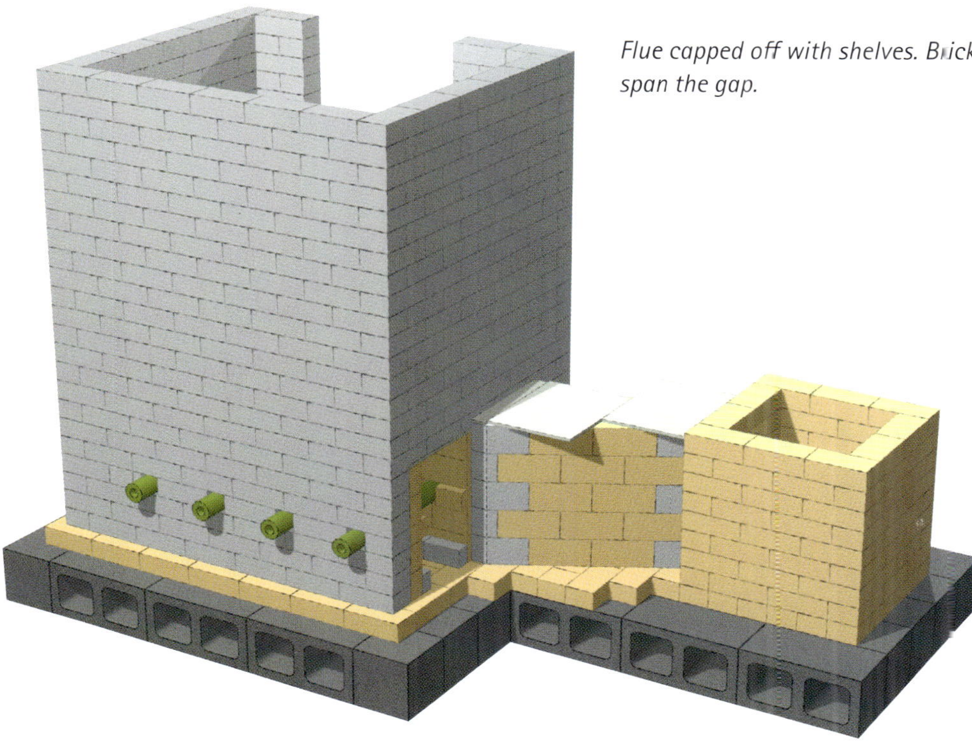

Flue capped off with shelves. Bricks can be used if they span the gap.

13 First spy hole brick cut on right-hand side.

14 View showing chimney, flue and wicket. Please note that the chimney base shown in the photographs here differs slightly from the original design shown in the diagrams, as it was built wider and narrower in order to accomodate Bob Park's double metal chimney (see p.76).

15 Geoff Cox and myself building up the chamber walls.

16 Kiln corner ironwork and arch former in place.

17 View from other side, also showing the two spy holes.

18 View from another angle.

19 Detail of the flue to the chimney showing the gap formed for the loose bricks that will be used as the passive damper and for closing off the kiln at the end of the firing.

20 Detail showing skewback (springer brick) and first four rows of side arch bricks over the arch former, supported on wooden posts.

21 View of inside the kiln showing the wooden posts supporting the arch former and the arch bricks in place.

22 The same view with the arch former removed.

23 View showing ironwork, including thrust bar supporting arch.

Oval dish by Jce Finch, fired in similar wood-fired kiln.

24 Ceramic fibre laid over arch.

Ironwork in place with arch completed and chimney half built. From this height the chimney can be built to it's full height with common house bricks, (and the ironwork should also continue to the top).

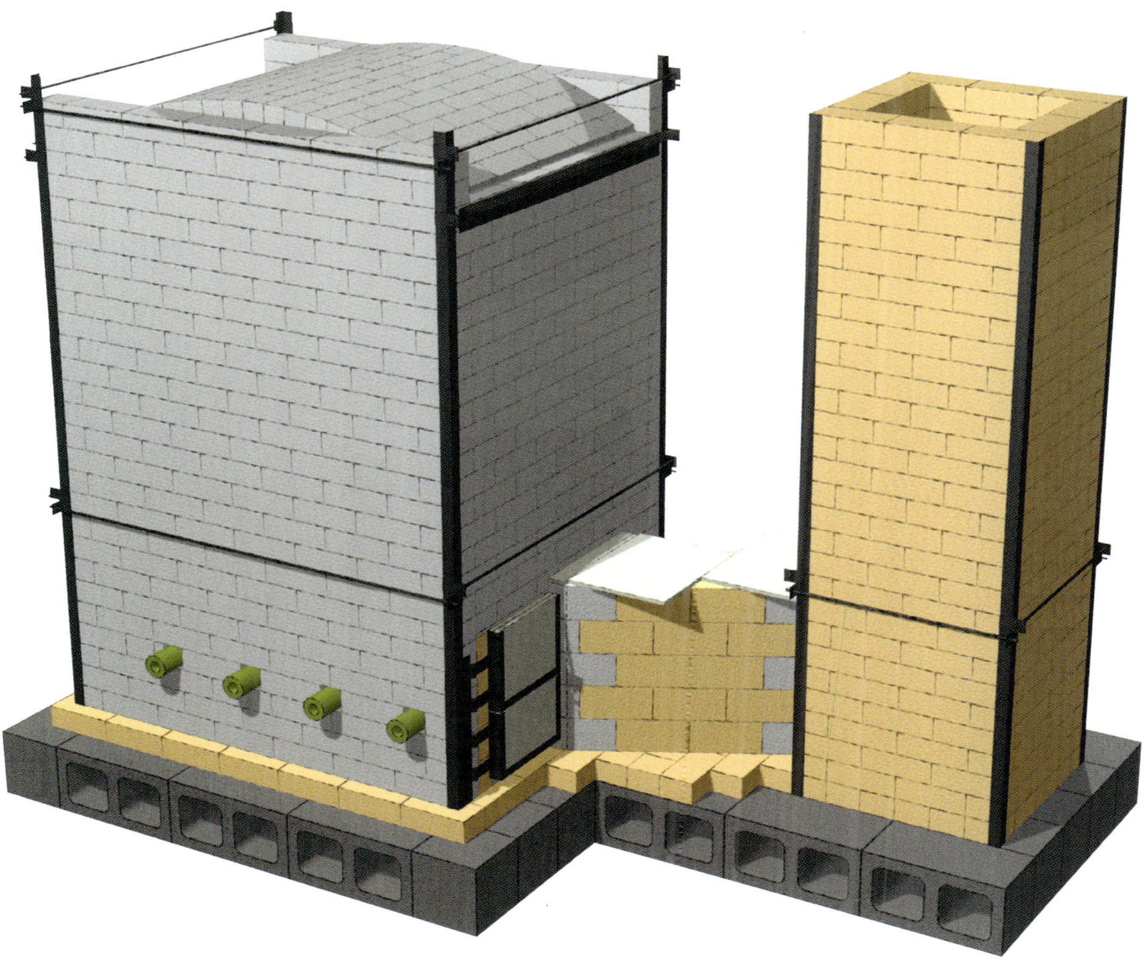

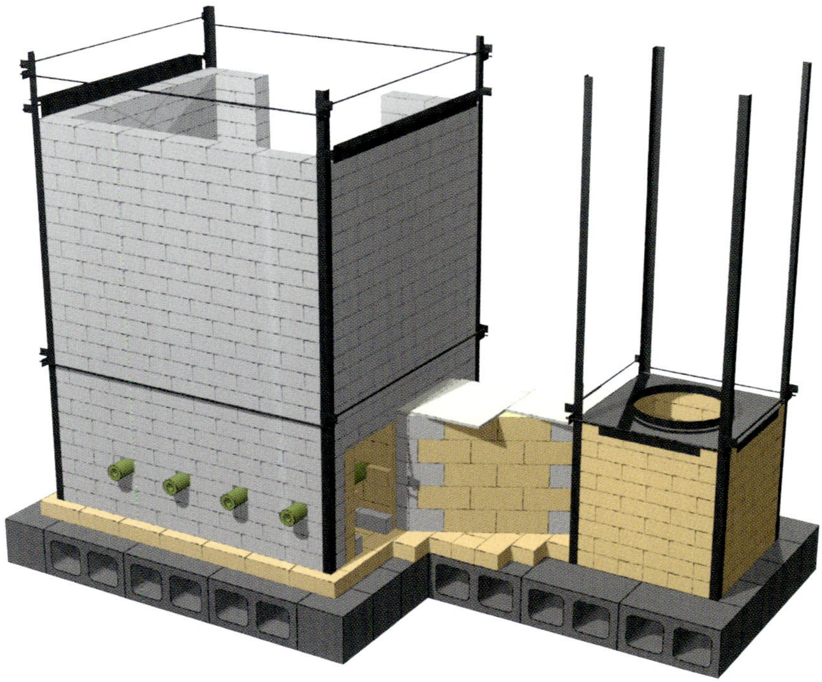

An alternative chimney arrangement, fitting a metal collar rather than building completely from bricks.

Metal chimney in place. The chimney would need to be higher than is shown in this diagram.

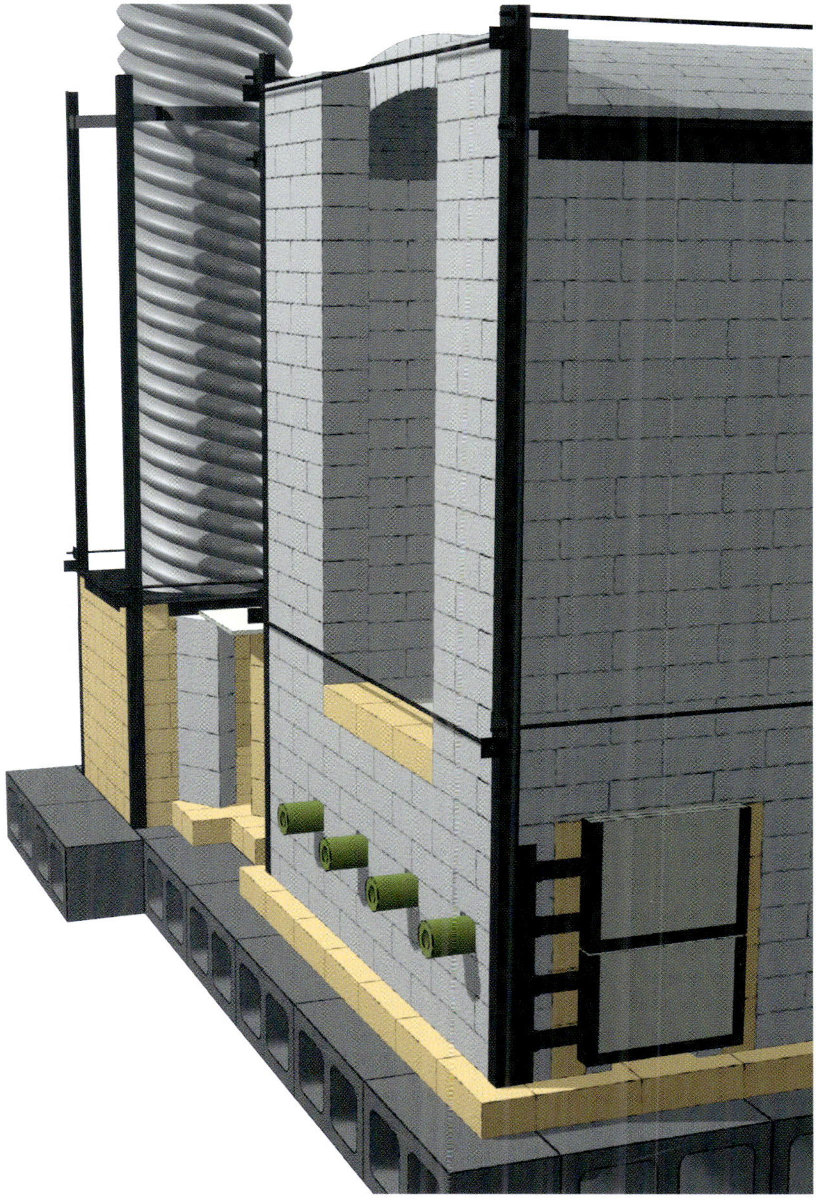

View from wicket side of the kiln.

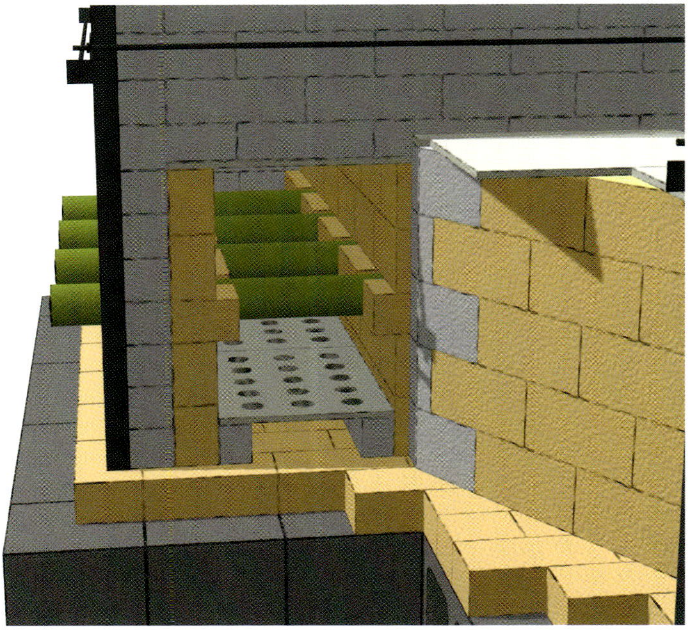

Detail of one of the fireboxes before fitting the firebox doors, showing the perforated shelves and the firebars in position.

25 and 26 Detail of the metal stable doors for the fireboxes.

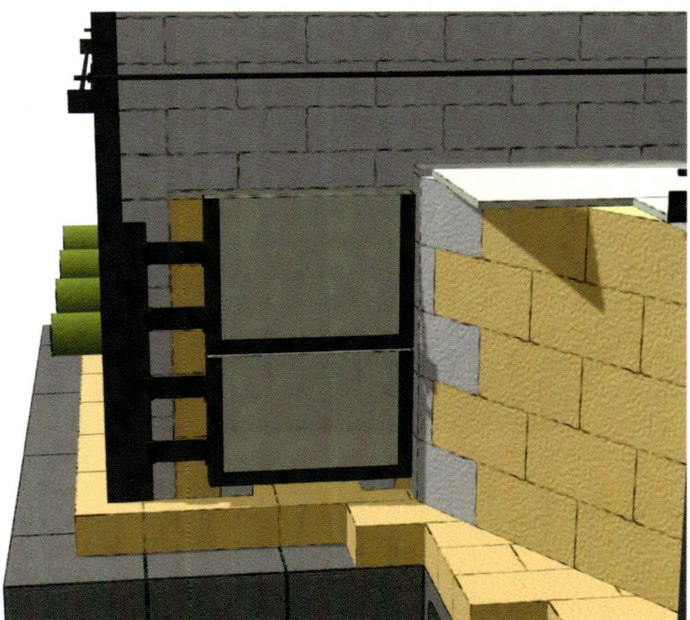

Detail showing firebox 'stable doors'.

27 A sandwich of kiln shelves and fibre are fitted into the metal channel of the door frames.

28 Laying out the first kiln shelves ready for packing. The shelves underneath, which form the top of the fireboxes, are covered with ceramic fibre to insulate the chamber from the cold air entering the fireboxes. The gap shown at the top right (and part shown at bottom left) is where the flame enters the kiln.

29 Kiln packed ready for Bob Park's first firing in the new wood-fired kiln.

30 Rockwool insulation (foil backed cavity batts) fitted to outside of kiln.

31 Graham Taylor closing firebox door after stoking.

First firing of Bob Park's kiln taking place. This view shows the 23cm (9in.) twin metal chimneys he used in place of a single 46cm (18in.) chimney shown in the previous diagrams.

Bowl by Bob Park.

KILN LOG

Monday 17/08/03 – Firing 127 (raw glaze stoneware) – Damp – Low cloud – Light wind from south-west

Two burners on low from 11pm night before for pre-heat. Flue control: 3 bricks out of chimney flue.

Start firing at 5am. Set 'kiln clock' to 00:00 As I am firing with wood and need to be with the kiln the whole time I take temperature readings every 15 minutes. All temperature readings are in °C.

Time	°C	Comment
00:00	150	Turn up gas burners. Short wood on firebox floor at front of fireboxes.
00:15	180	
00:30	200	Short wood on floor and on firebars at front of fireboxes.
00:45	230	
01:00	270	All wood on top of firebars. Gas burners turned low.
01:15	340	Long wood on firebars at front. Gas burners out.
01:30	390	
01:45	410	Long wood on firebars, back of fireboxes.
02:00	440	Two bricks back in flue to increase pull to chimney. 1 brick out.
02:15	490	
02:30	500	All bricks in.
02:45	550	
03:00	565	
03:15	615	
03:30	660	
03:45	685	
04:00	725	
04:15	755	
04:30	785	
04:45	805	
05:00	845	
05:15	860	
05:30	890	
05:45	905	
06:00	915	
06:15	940	
06:30	950	
06:45	970	
07:00	975	
07:15	980	Very light stoking with thin wood to hold temperature.
07:30	990	Very light stoking with thin wood to hold temperature.
07:45	995	Very light stoking with thin wood to hold temperature.
08:00	1000	Very light stoking with thin wood to hold temperature.
08:15	1000	Very light stoking with thin wood to hold temperature.
08:30	1000	Very light stoking with thin wood to hold temperature.
08:45	995	Very light stoking with thin wood to hold temperature.
09:00	1000	Cone 06 down. – Start reduction – heavy stoking. 2 bricks out.
09:15	1020	
09:30	1035	
09:45	1045	
10:00	1055	
10:15	1075	
10:30	1085	
10:45	1095	
11:00	1105	
11:15	1120	
11:30	1130	
11:45	1145	
12:00	1155	
12:15	1160	
12:30	1170	
12:45	1180	
13:00	1185	
13:15	1190	
13:30	1200	
13:45	1210	
14:00	1215	
14:15	1220	Cone 9 bending. Pyro reading low, real temperature approx. 1260°C.
14:30	1225	
14:45	1230	
15:00	1235	Cone 9 down cone 10 bending. Temperature approx. 1275°C.
15:15	1240	
15:30	1250	Cones 9 & 10 down 11 bending. Temperature approx. 1300°C.
15:45	1250	
16:00	1255	Cones 9, 10 & 11 down. Temp. approx. 1310°C. Stop stoking. All bricks out.
16:15	1202	Open firebox doors for crash cool.
16:30	1150	Close firebox doors. Shut slide damper to chimney. Clam up.

Wood and Gas Kiln

(With ports for using soda. Could use oil burners in place of the gas.)

'The kiln that Joe designed for me is the most interesting I have ever had and is very efficient. It allows me to fire with purely gas or gas and wood. I have gradually increased the amount of wood that I use so that there is a visual difference in the surface of the pots.

It is a great pleasure to fire, with a very even temperature throughout. The double flue [the central flues in base of kiln] is a feature which I particularly appreciate. It allows me to direct the flame either to the front or to the back of the kiln, if it is necessary to bring the temperature up in either place. I love using wood but am not in a position to fire with wood exclusively, so this kiln goes some way to fulfilling my desire to wood fire but with the help of propane gas.'

Ruthanne Tudball

Prepare a flat level base large enough for the kiln and chimney.

1 If using concrete blocks, place them without mortar, to cover the kiln and chimney area. Small gaps of up to 5cm (2in.) between the blocks are acceptable.

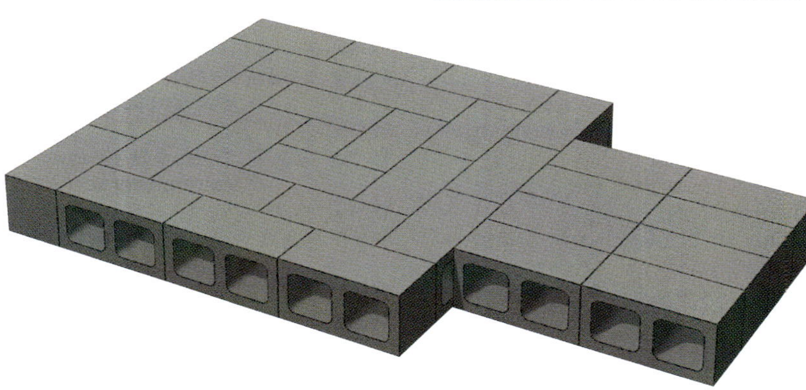

2 Cover the top surface of the blocks or concrete with a layer of ceramic fibre paper or blanket.

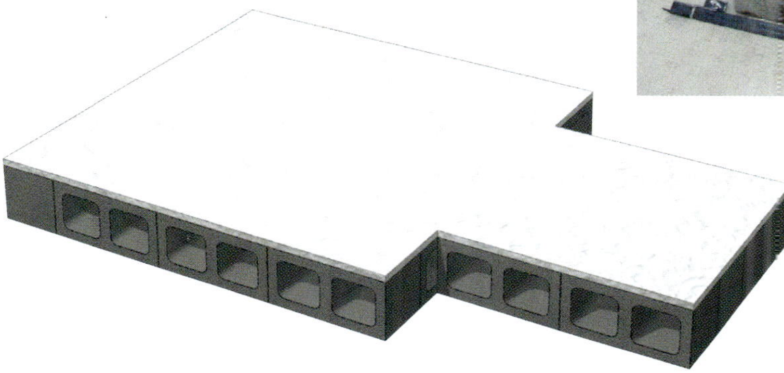

Ceramic blanket over concrete blocks.

If you are not using blocks and the concrete base is being laid new it is a wise precaution to drill holes every 15–20cm (6–8in.) over the area of kiln and chimney. (If you can drill the concrete before it sets hard the job is easily done.) This is to allow any steam that may be produced in the concrete during firing, to escape.

3 Place a layer of firebricks over the ceramic fibre. The foundations or base is now complete and you are ready to start the kiln construction.

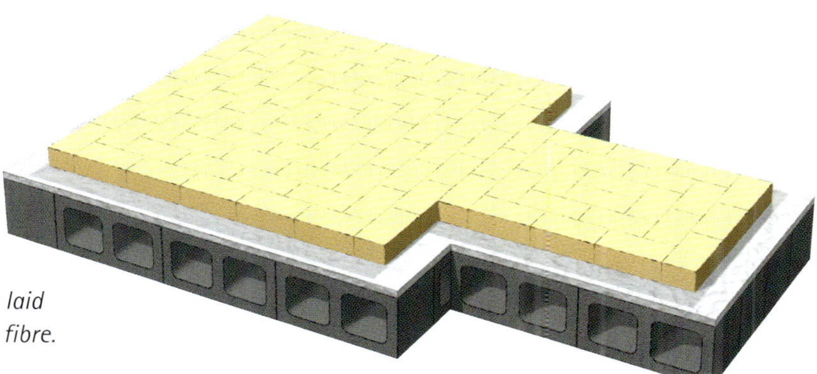

Layer of firebricks laid on top of ceramic fibre.

4 Layer 1 of the kiln is placed, forming the outer walls, fireboxes, flues and chimney base. The width of the fireboxes is approximately 15cm (6in.) and the exit flues 13m (5in.) Gaps of 5cm (2in.) are left either side of the chimney flue that will be used as passive dampers and for the slide damper.

Expansion slots should be allowed between every two bricks. These can be filled with ceramic paper (2mm or 3mm/⅛in. thickness) cut 11.2cm × 7.5cm (4½ × 3in.). Check the kiln is square by measuring diagonally from corner to corner, both ways should be the same.

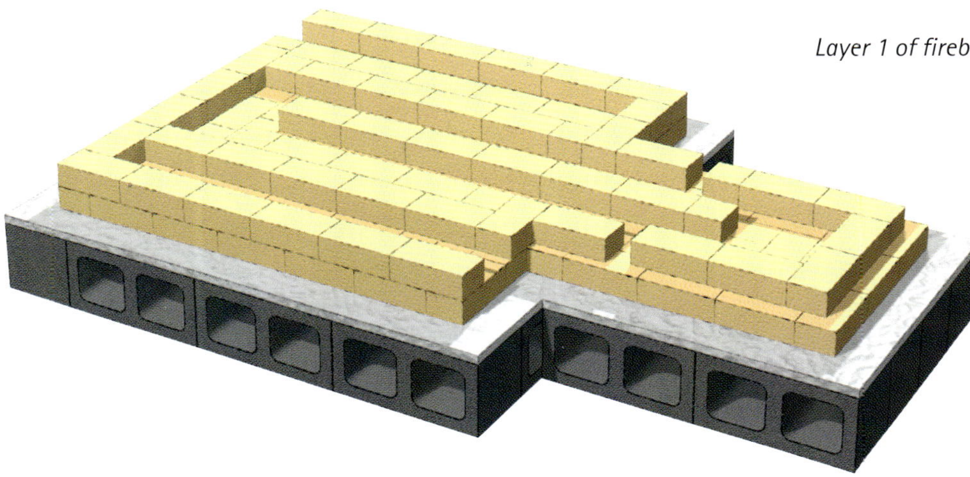

Layer 1 of firebricks.

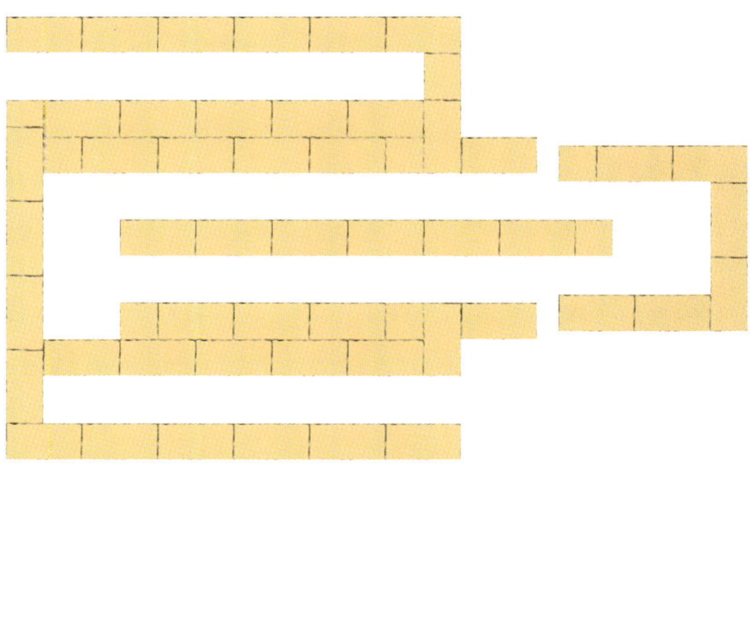

Plan of Layer 1.

5 Layer 3 goes on.

6 Layer 4, having bricked over the top of the burner ports, work starts on the chimney flue.

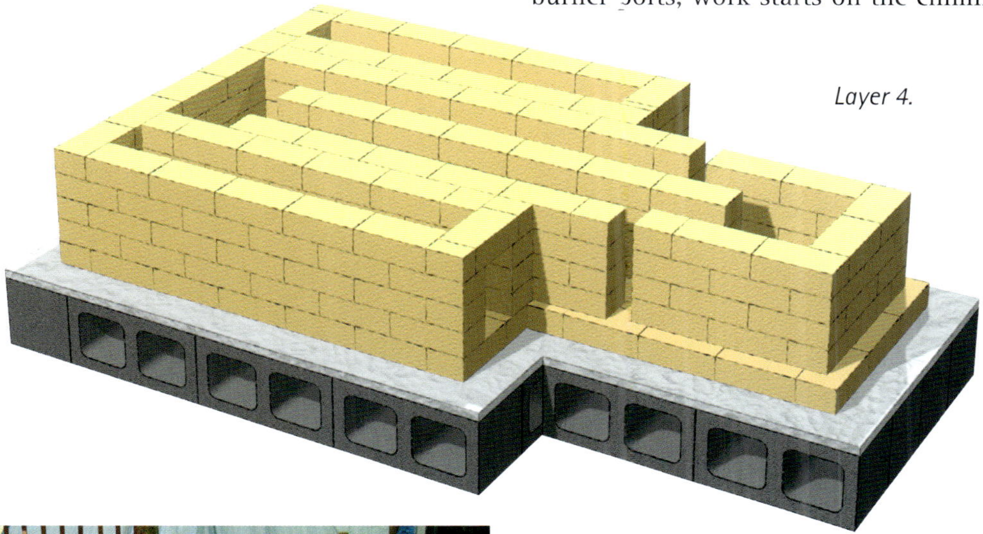

Layer 4.

7 Layer 5, 7.5cm (3in.) diameter firebars are put into position. They protrude from the walls so they can be removed and replaced during firing, should one get broken. The top of the second internal flue and both exit flues to the chimney are capped off with bricks. Gaps are filled with cut insulating bricks or ceramic fibre.

Layer 5.

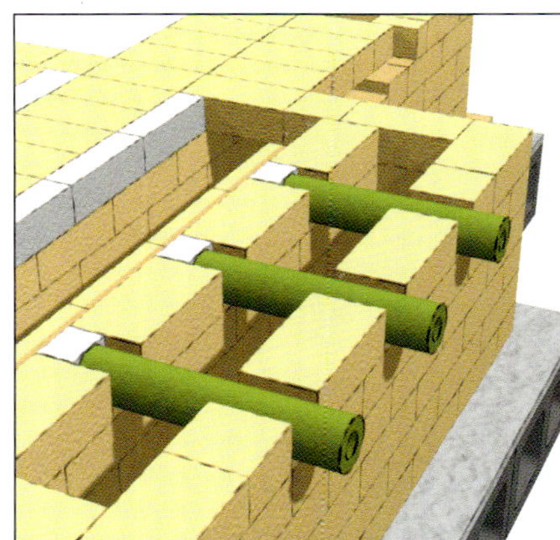

Detail of layer 5.

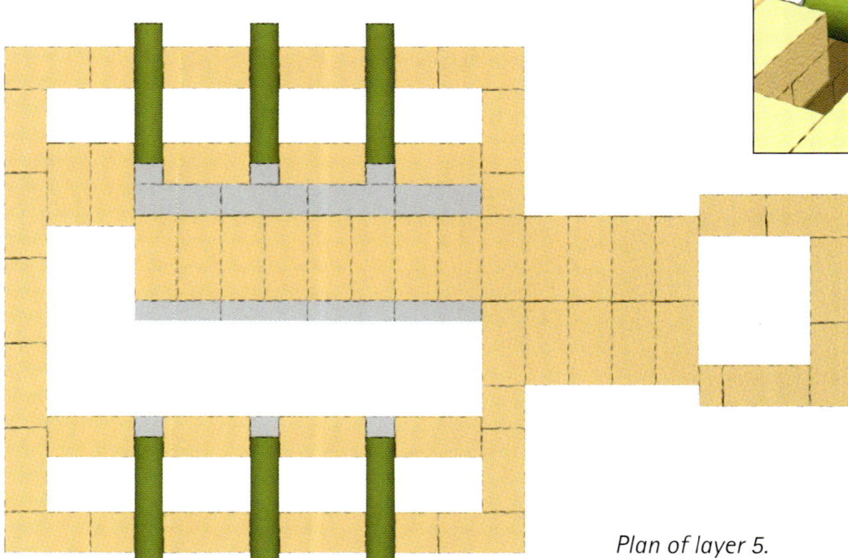

Plan of layer 5.

8 Fireboxes and outer walls continue, leaving gaps for the stoke-holes.

9 The chimney bricks are corbelled in to form the correct chimney area. Note the gap in the flue between the chamber and the chimney. This is for the slide damper. There is another the same on the opposite side.

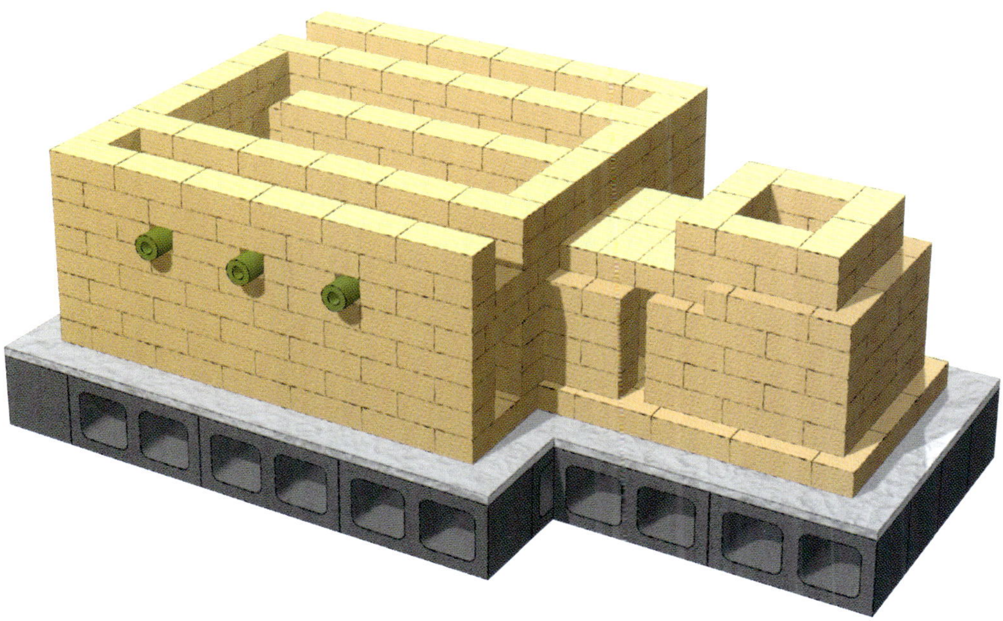

Chimney corbelled in to form finished dimensions.

The kiln shelves that form the base of the firing chamber are put in position. (When packing the kiln the front two can be removed to allow space to step inside the kiln so aiding the packing of the back two shelves.) The first layer of insulating bricks are placed. Note the gap left that will form the wicket (doorway).

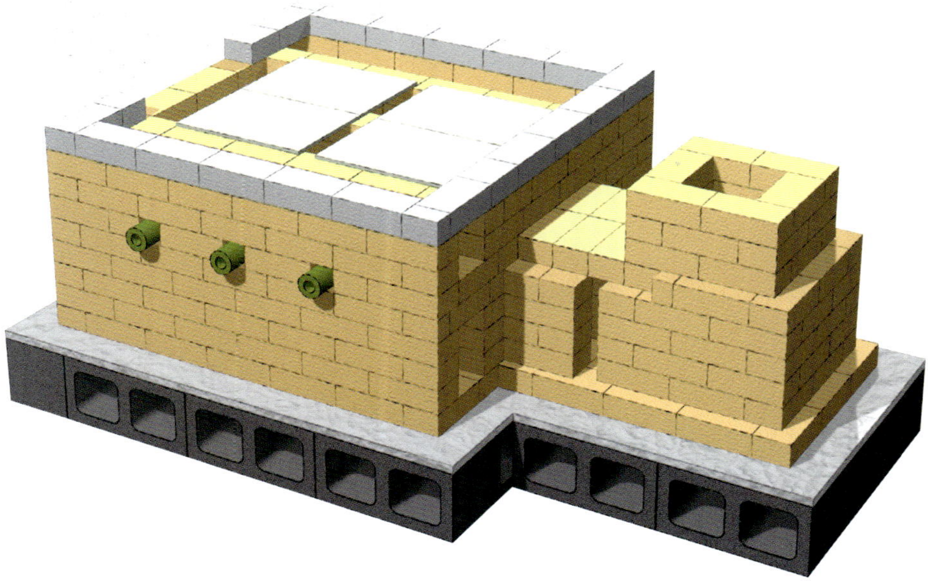

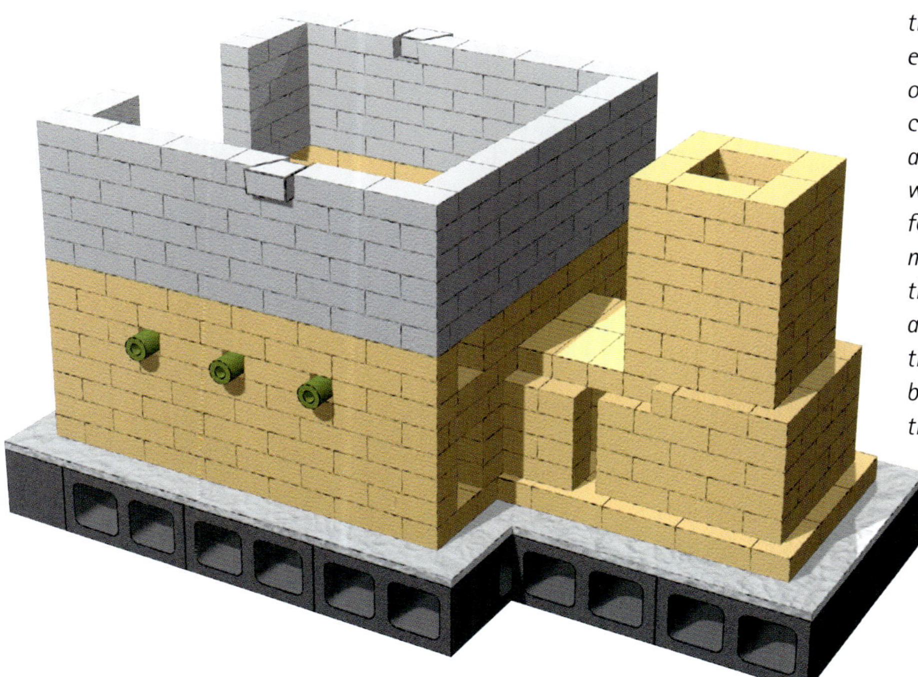

View showing the cut bricks that make up the spy holes on either side (for viewing cones or spraying soda). Spy holes can be made in this way on any layer or position in the walls of the kiln should you feel you may need them. It is much easier to build them in than to try and make spy holes after the kiln is finished. If they are not needed they can be left closed and not affect the kiln or firing.

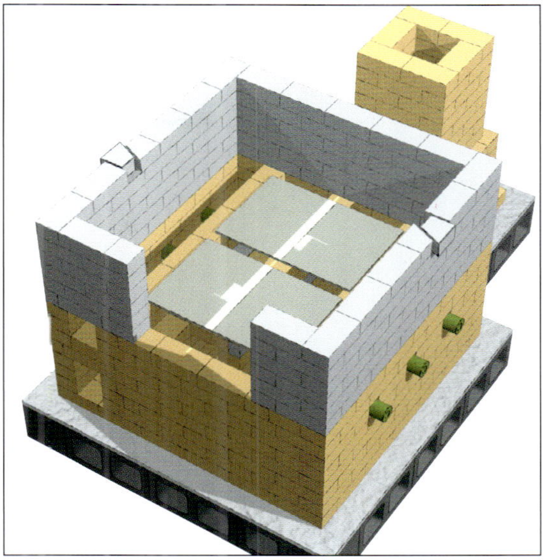

RIGHT View from front of kiln showing the spy holes and wicket (doorway) being formed.

BELOW View showing the spy holes and the skewback bricks on the chamber walls ready for the arch construction.

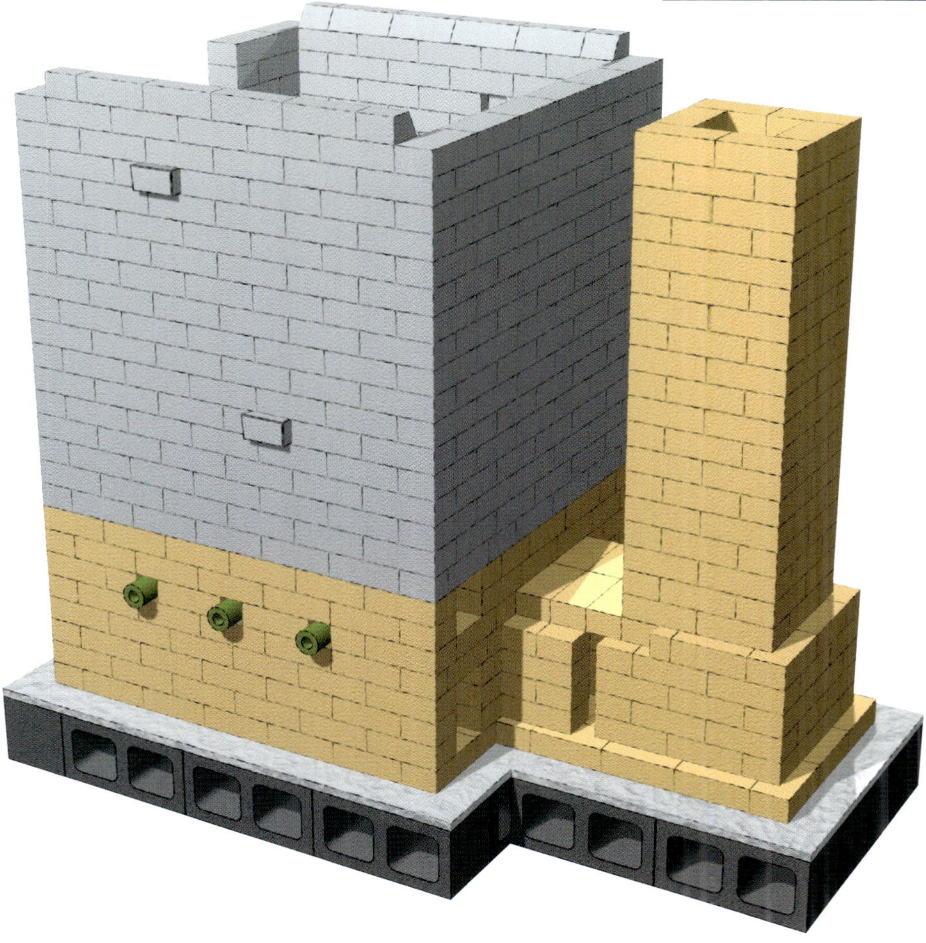

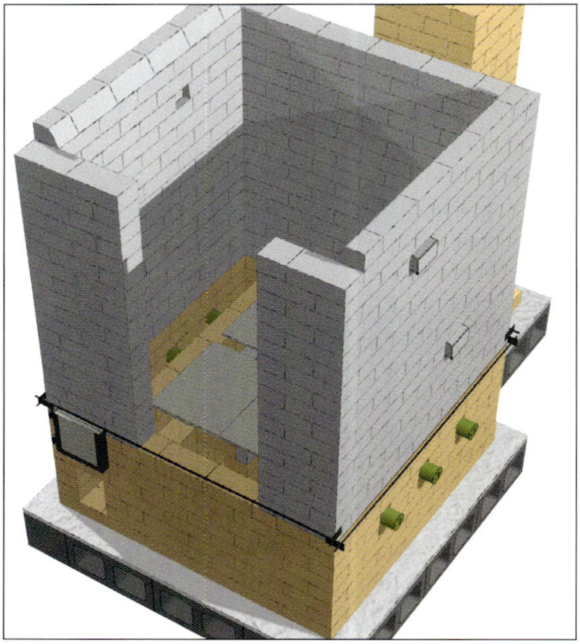

View from top front of kiln.

10 Starting to fit the ironwork. Ruthanne Tudball, Richard Godfrey and Kevin de Choisy assisting the kiln build.

11 Layer 13 with corner ironwork in place and the kiln building continuing within it. Showing front gas burner port at the bottom of the kiln with the wood stoke-hole above. The 'wicket' (doorway) is to the right with loose bricks filling the gap for the first 3 layers to check the width.

Detail of ironwork showing top firebox door fitted.

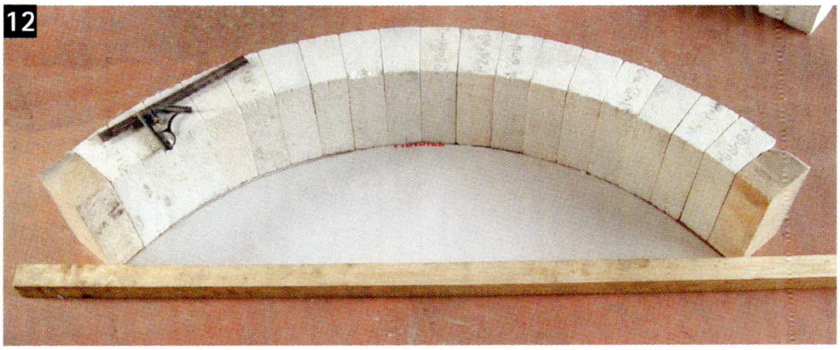

12 Working out the span, rise and skewbacks for the arch.

BELOW *The kiln ironwork is fitted and skewback bricks (springer bricks) are placed with the thrust irons supporting them.*

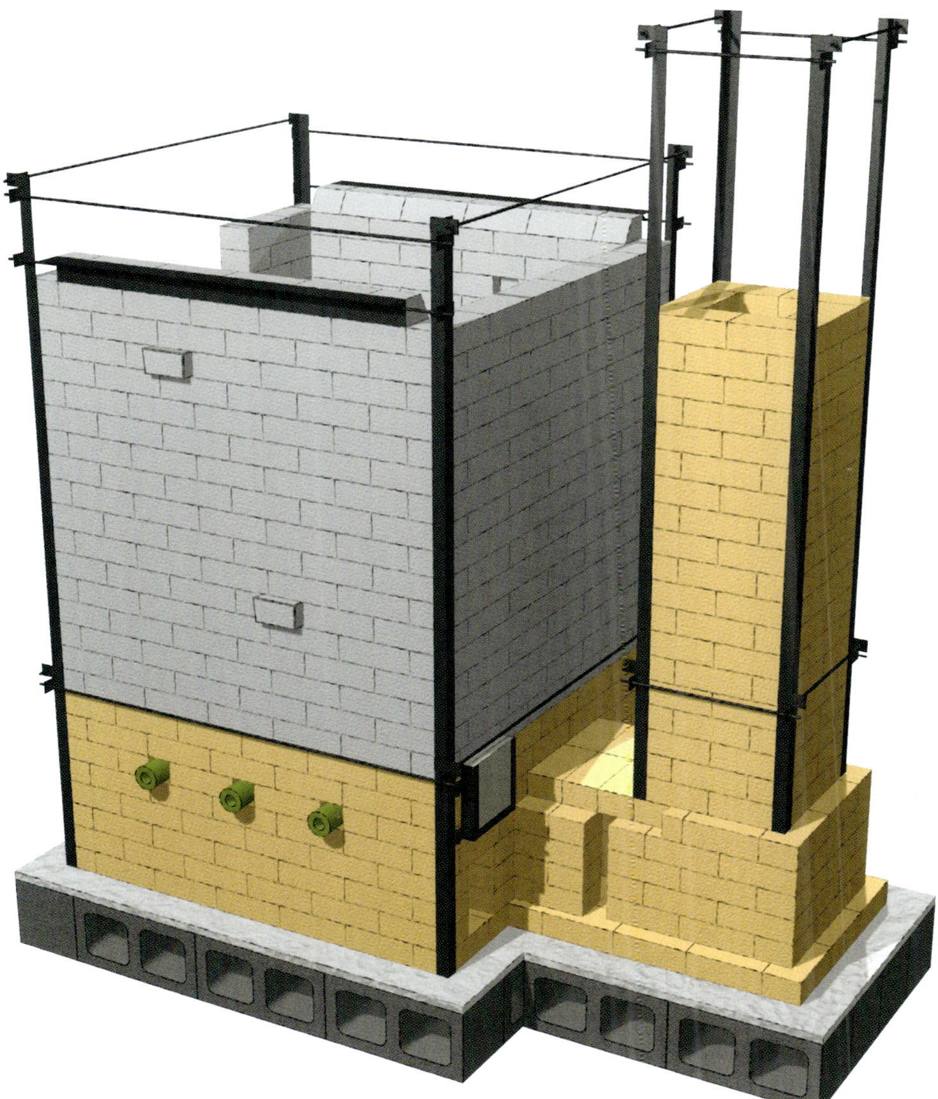

13 Arch former in place ready to start laying arch bricks.

14 Welding the thrust ironwork in place before removing the arch former.

15 Arch former removed.

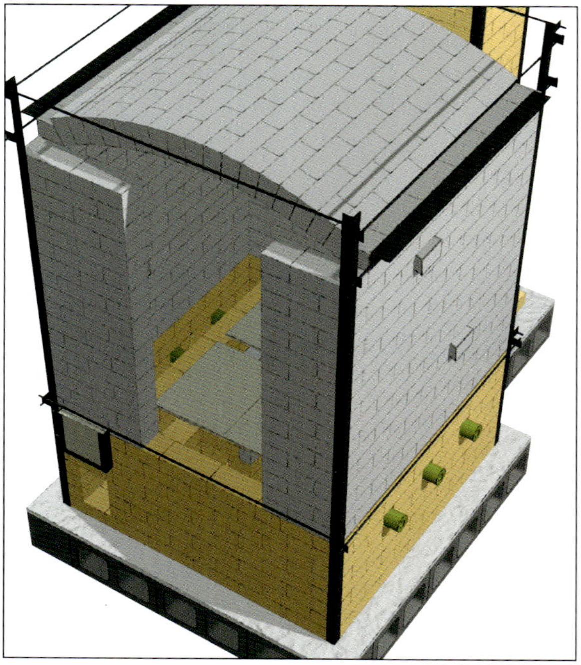

View from top front of kiln.

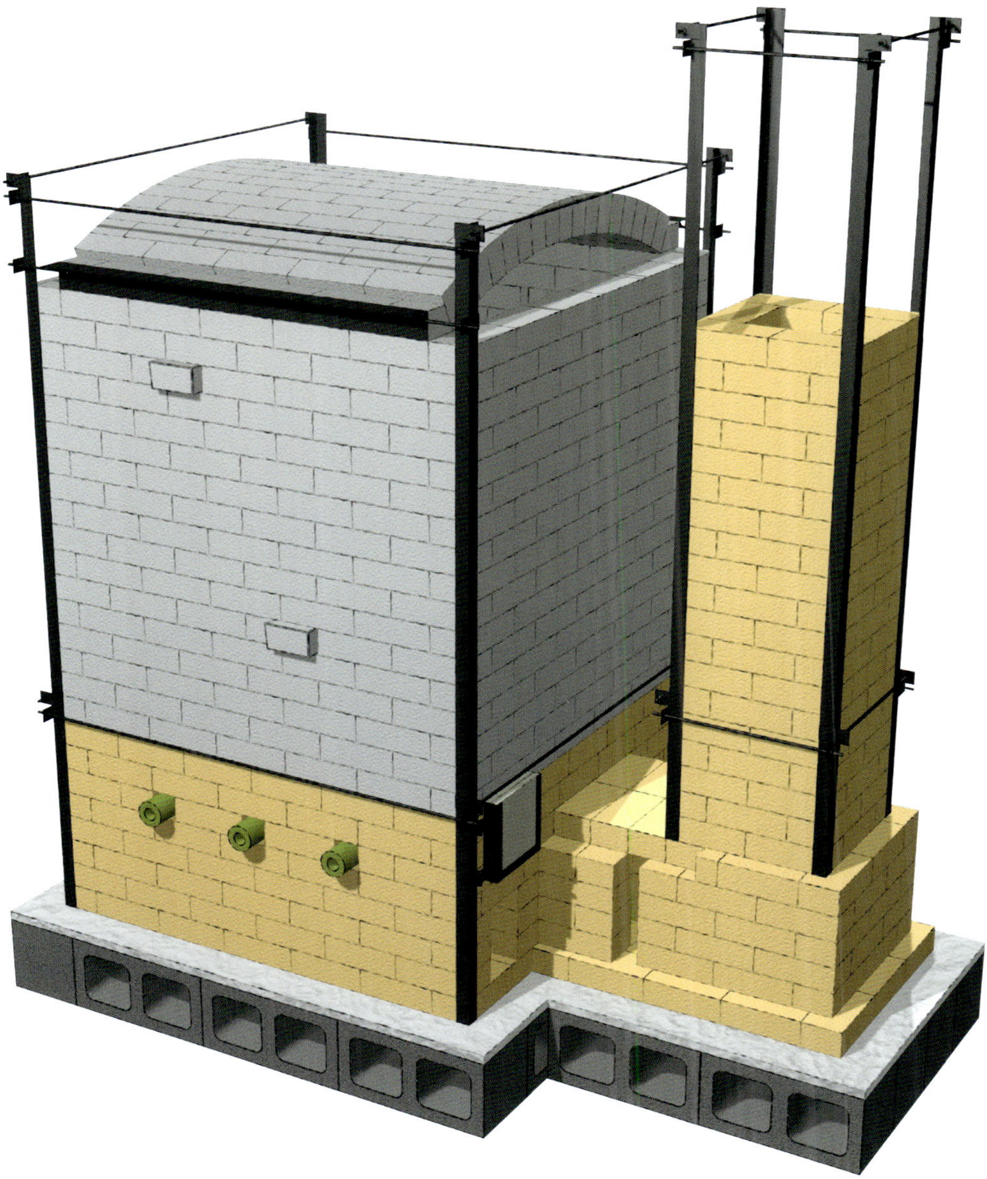

Arch completed with arch former removed. The back wall is still to be built up.

Front and back walls built up against the arch.

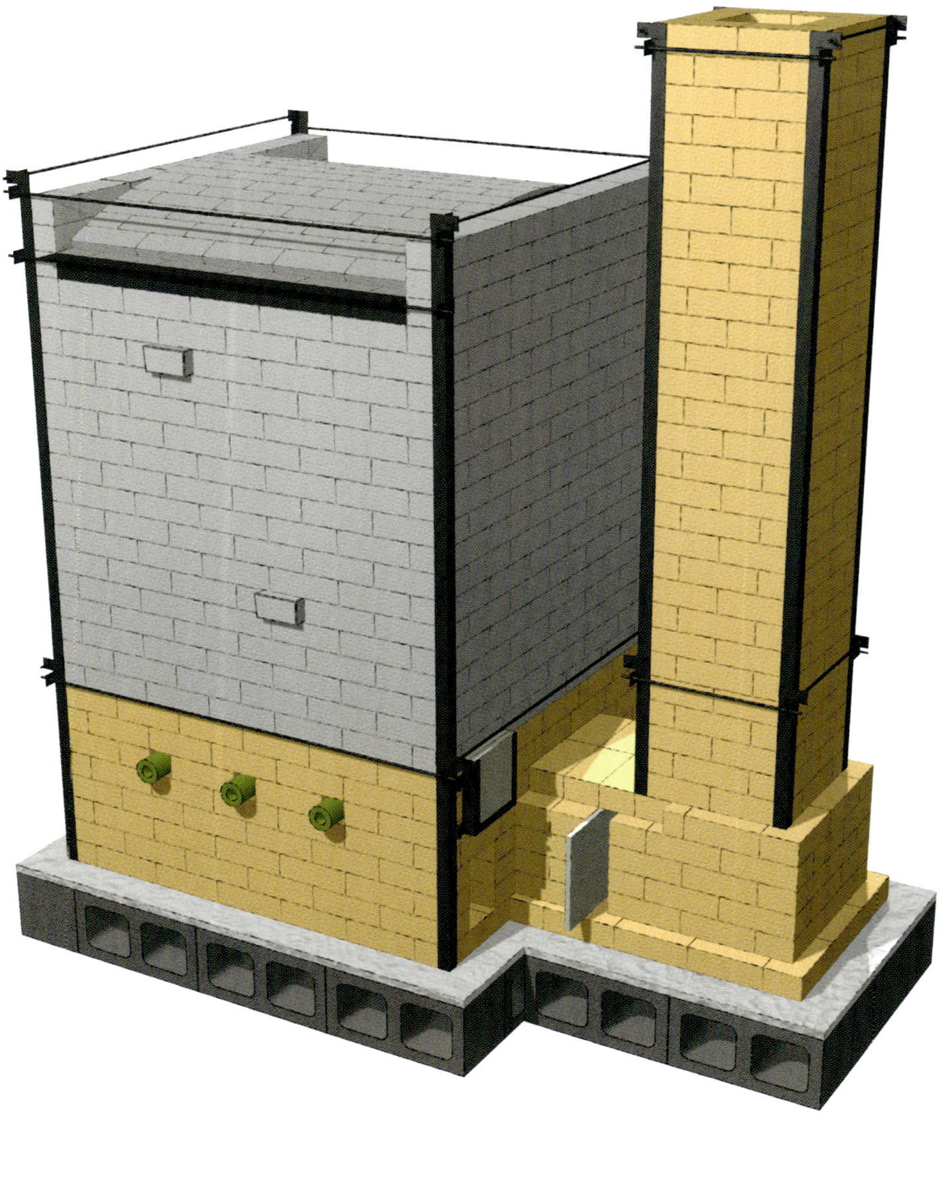

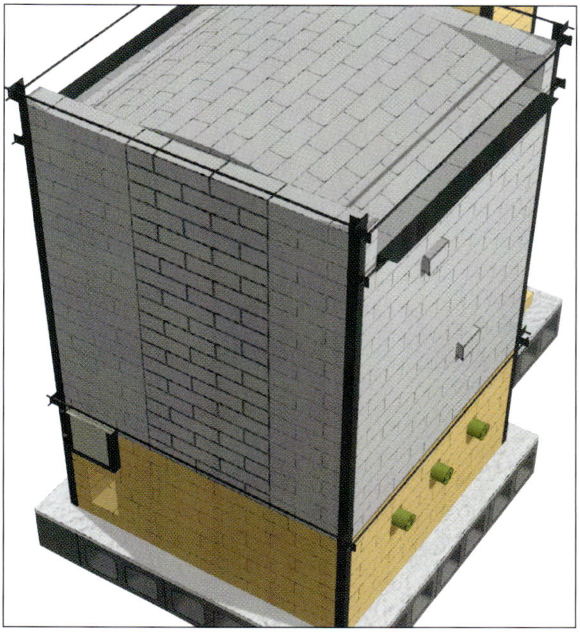

View showing the wicket bricks built up. Although not shown in this diagram I would recommend cutting three spy holes (high, middle and low) in the wicket.

16 Ruthanne Tudball packing the kiln for the first firing.

17 Gas burner on temporary stand.

18 The first firing half unpacked.

Ruthanne Tudball, pots and teapot from 2006 firing.

Gas Kiln

(Could be fired with Natural gas, LPG or oil.)

'Living in the centre of a small city has prevented me from having a salt or wood fired kiln. In addition to this I work from a studio within an arts centre where electricity was the only option for kiln firing. Due to this, in 1984 when I left college I changed from salt-firing white stoneware to making tin-glazed red earthenware and for the last 22 years I have had to be content with my electric kiln.

More recently, however, I have developed a new interest in making porcelain tableware with low relief surface patterns. This lead me to look more carefully at my stone built garden shed. Previously I had thought it too small to house a kiln, but after a clear out and a coat of white paint it proved to be just large enough.

I had not built or fired a propane kiln for over two decades and so I was extremely lucky to employ Joe Finch to design and build a small soda kiln with me. Although I knew that I could build one myself, I remembered from my student days that poorly designed kilns can struggle to reach temperature, fire unevenly and give little chance of achieving consistent good results, so I was very happy to rely on Joe's long experience and genius for kiln design.

By obtaining all of the materials in advance the kiln building only took us two days and the result was a beautiful little soda kiln. It has an internal packing space of 68cm (26¼in.) high up to the start of the arch and the arch goes up a further 10cm (4in.) to 78cm (30½in.) high. The packing space is 46cm (18in.) wide by 83cm (32½in.) deep. This allows for two stacks of kiln shelves 46cm (18in.) long by 35.5cm (14in.) wide. The kiln fires very evenly and reduces readily when just one chimney bung is removed during the firing. The extra soda ports around the kiln enable an even coverage of soda on the pots. The last firing used approximately one 47 kilo bottle of liquid propane gas to fire the kiln in 14 hours to cone 10 including a one hour soak as the soda was sprayed in.

The size of the kiln enables me to pack and fire it easily without help. Although I have had only three firings in the kiln so far, I already have an enormous affection for my little kiln. It has given me the confidence to know that I will continue to enjoy the challenge of learning and understanding how to get the best results from each firing.'

Morgen Hall

Prepare a flat level base large enough for the kiln and chimney.

1 Lay out insulating bricks to mark the size and position of the kiln and chimney.

2 Place loose concrete blocks to cover the marked area.

If using concrete blocks, place them without mortar, to cover the kiln and chimney area. Small gaps of up to 5cm (2in.) between the blocks are acceptable.

3 The blocks are covered with two layers of ceramic paper (3mm/⅛in. thick).

4 A rectangle of firebricks are placed marking the outside measurements of the kiln. The firebricks used in the photographs of this kiln were an odd size measuring 34.2 × 11.4 × 7.6cm (13.5 × 4.5 × 3in.). The bricks in the diagrams are the standard 23 × 11.4 × 7.6cm (9 × 4.5 × 3in.).

5 Covering the fibre with a layer of firebricks.

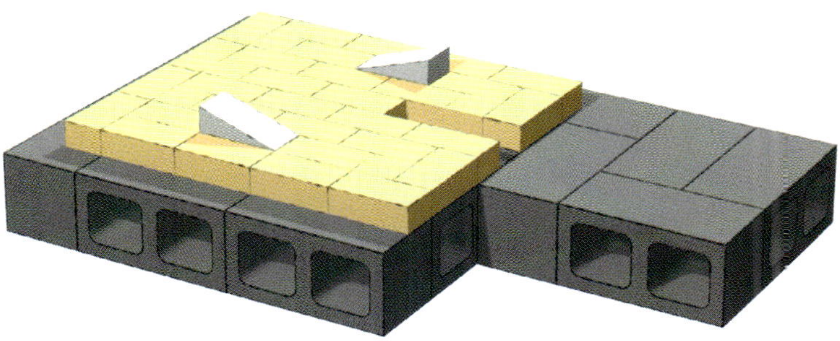

Firebricks laid dry. The two cut insulating bricks shown in this diagram would be placed later in the fireboxes but are shown here as it is difficult to see them once the firebox walls are built.

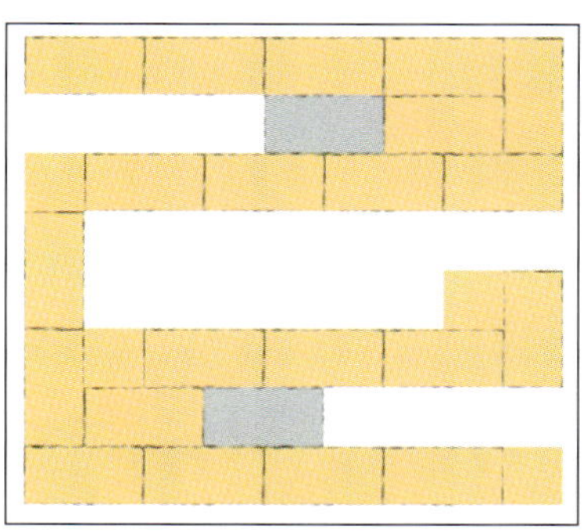

Plan of layer 2.

6 Fireboxes, central flue and chimney being formed.

7

8

7 & 8 Adding firebars (30cm × 4.5cm/12in. × 1¾in. tubular props) should you wish to end the firing with some wood. If you want simply a gas kiln then these firebars, and the firebox openings should be ignored.

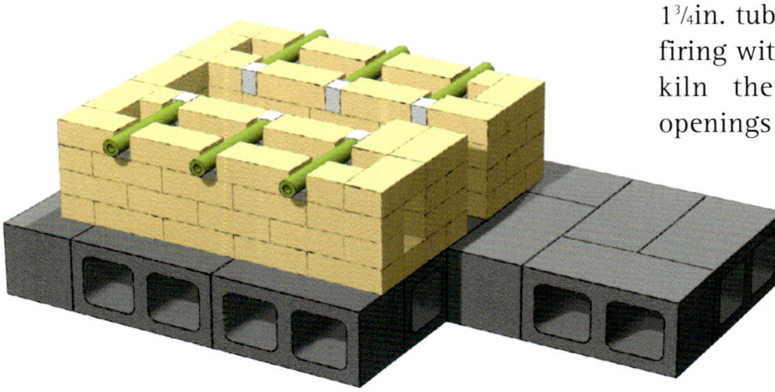

Adding firebars.

9

10

9 Gaps are filled with cut insulating bricks and ceramic fibre.

10 The top of firebox walls are covered with a layer of ceramic paper to act as a gasket before starting the kiln chamber walls.

Fireboxes completed. The bottom holes are for the burners with the above holes being the stoke-holes for wood.

Chamber walls started with first two layers of insulating bricks.

11 Building the chamber walls with insulating bricks.

12 Ironwork fitted to kiln.

13 Birds eye view of chimney and chamber.

14 Morgen cutting a hole in the tin roof for the chimney.

15 The angle of the skewback is marked on cardboard which is then cut and used as a template.

16 Cutting a skewback brick with a saw.

17 The cut skewback is tested with the arch bricks.

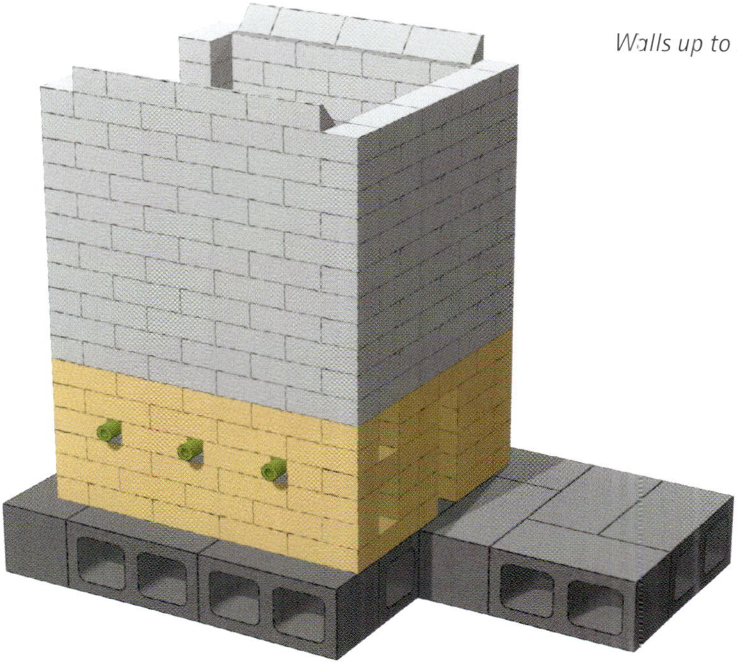

Walls up to skewback level.

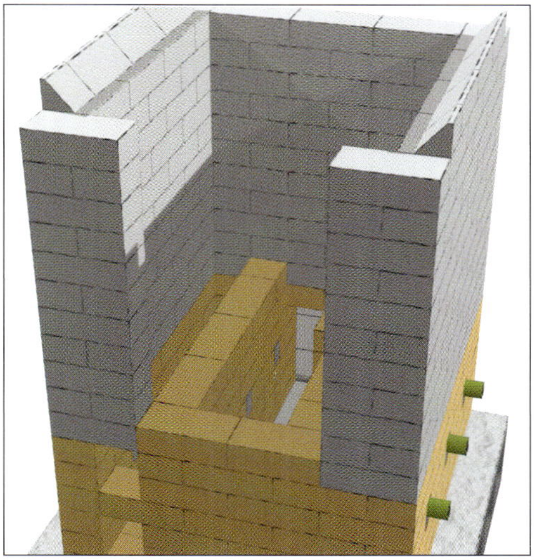

View from wicket.

18 View inside kiln showing arch former supported with wooden posts.

Ironwork in place.

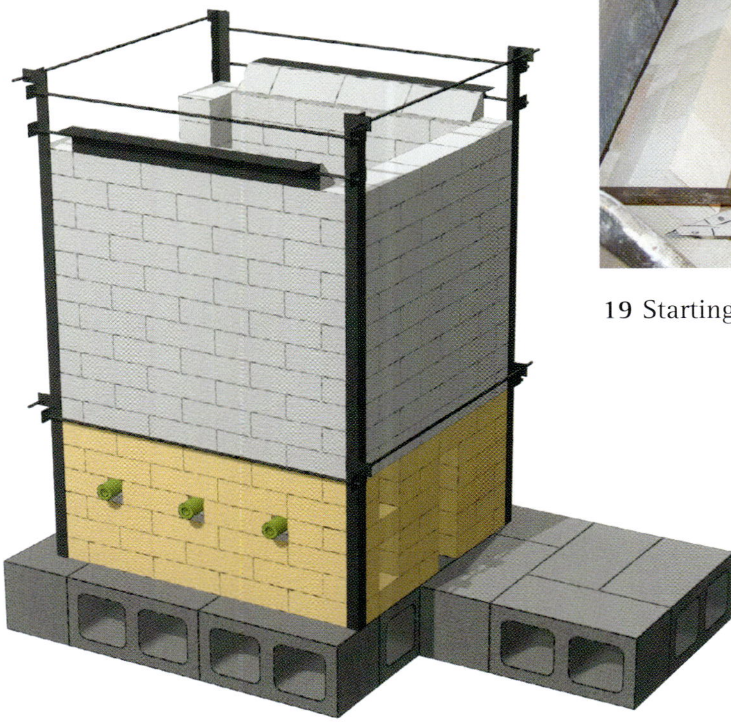

19 Starting to lay the arch bricks.

20 Arch nearly complete.

21 View from the wicket.

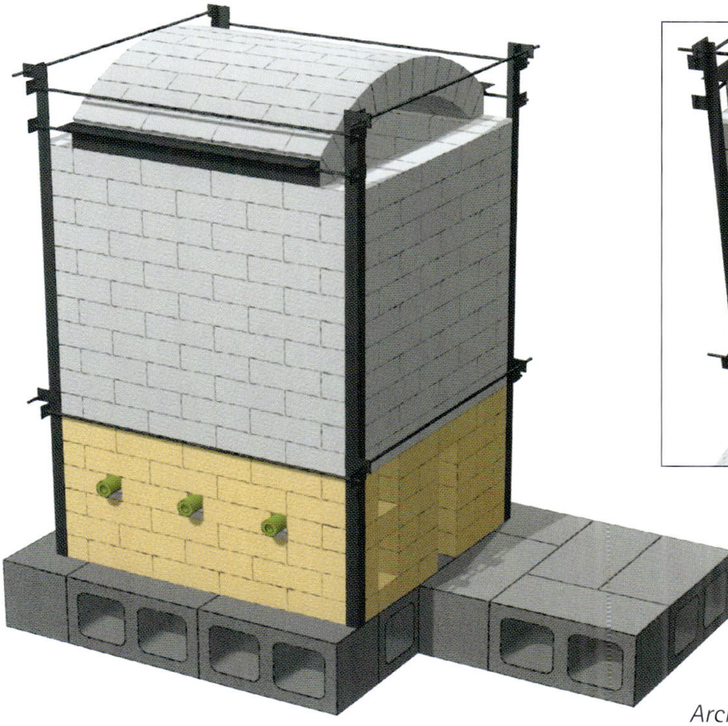

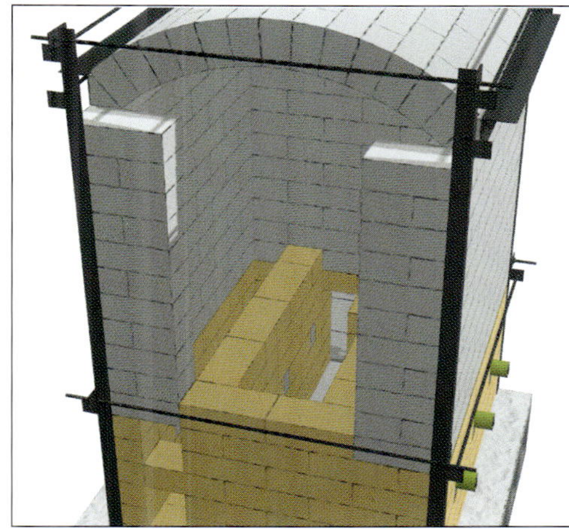

View from wicket.

Arch completed.

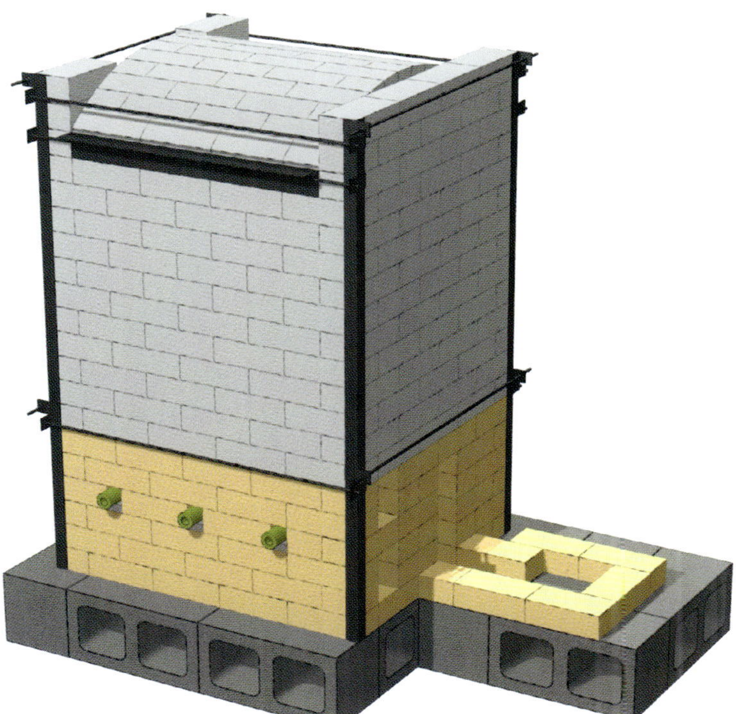

Side walls of kiln completed and chimney started.

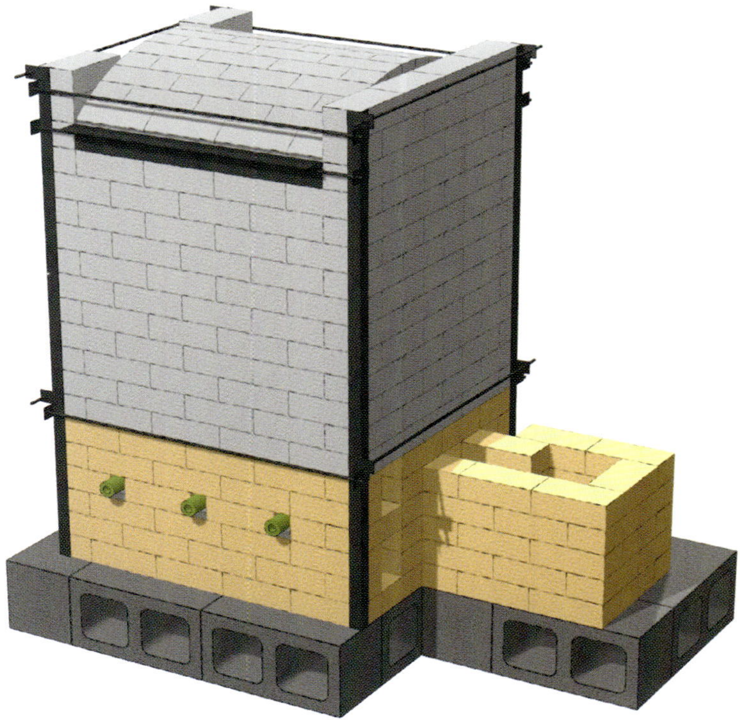

Chimney continuing.

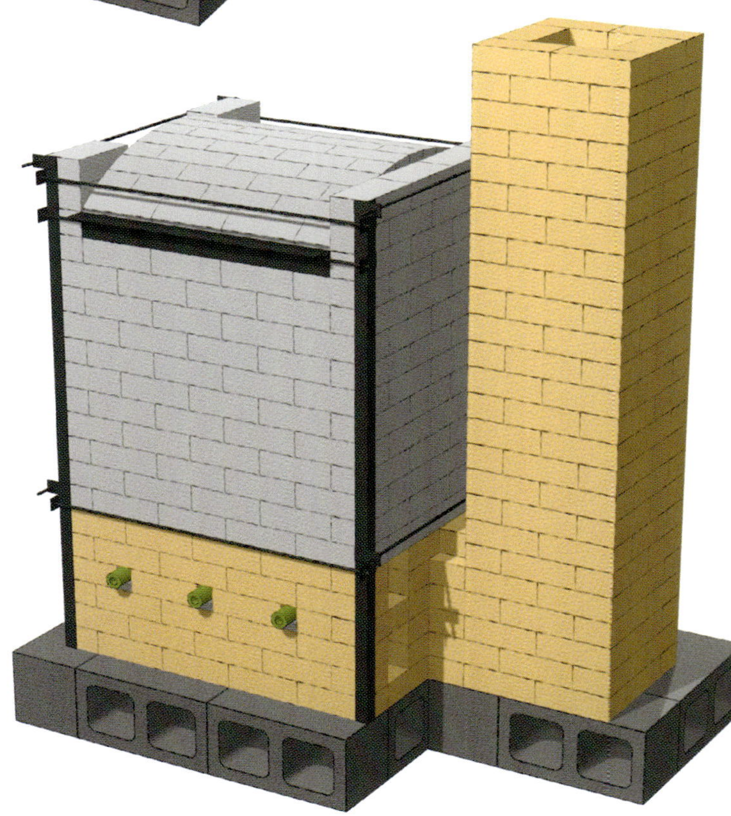

Three quarters of the chimney built.

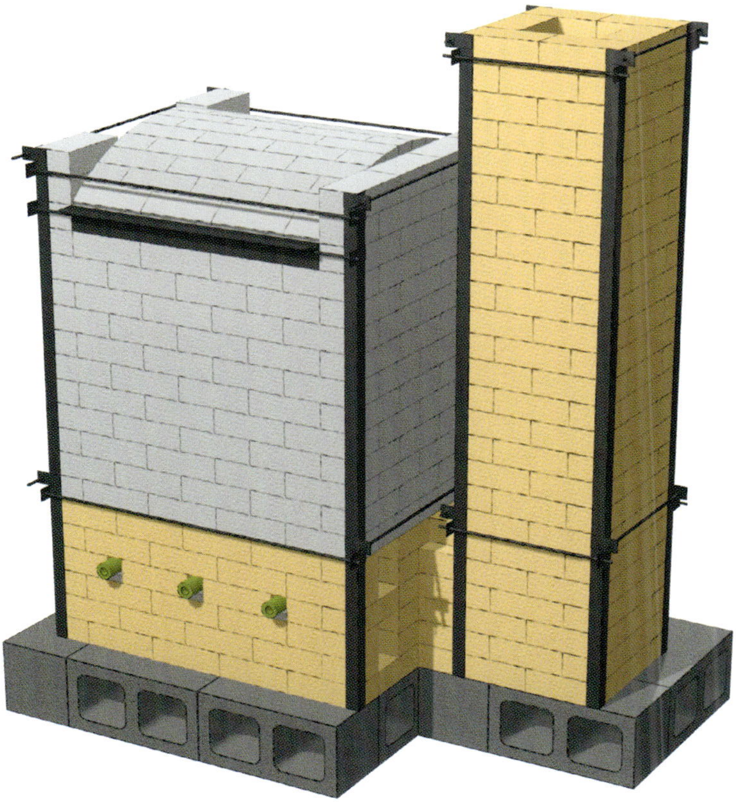

Ironwork around chimney. A further 10 to 15 courses need to be added to complete the chimney, with the ironwork extending to the top of the chimney.

22 Kiln and chimney ironwork in place.

23 View inside kiln. The wedge shaped bricks (waste pieces of brick, they do not need to be cut this shape) are to stop the flames from the fireboxes taking a shortcut under the shelves.

24 The first of the kiln shelves in position ready for packing.

25 Kiln wrapped with ceramic fibre and tin foil.

26 Front burner in operation. This was for the first firing and the burners were in a temporary position as the burner clamp had not been constructed.

27 An alternative method of fixing a burner to the kiln which allows the burner to move up and down and in and out. With this type of burner the metal sleeve on the barrel of the burner is also movable to help to produce a reduction flame.

Ram-pressed plate by Morgen Hall, soda glazed in the kiln.

Morgen Hall mug from first firing.

Results of the first firing in a gas kiln of the same design built for the Scottish Potters Association.

Appendix of Kiln Materials

Wood-fired kiln

Approximate list of materials used:

45 Concrete blocks
350 Firebricks
600 Insulating bricks
110 side arch bricks
150 Common house bricks
8 Firebars (good to have at least 2 extra for spares)
Perforated shelves, for firebox floors
8 300mm x 460mm kiln shelves, for roof of fireboxes.
4 rolls of 3660mm x 610mm x 50mm ceramic blanket.

Ironwork:
(The following are approximate sizes. Actual sizes should be measured from the kiln.)

4 1600mm tie rods (with nuts and washers to fit).
4 1370mm tie rods (with nuts and washers to fit).
4 2210mm x 50mm corner angle-irons for kiln.
4 2210mm x 50mm corner angle-irons for lower part of the chimney.
4 2210mm x 50mm corner angle-irons for upper part of the chimney.
2 1090mm x 75mm angle-iron thrust bars.
Sufficient iron to make up firebox doors.

Wood and gas kiln

Approximate list of materials used:

35 Concrete blocks
520 Firebricks
350 Insulating bricks
110 side arch bricks
Common house bricks, enough to take the chimney up to the required height.
6 Firebars (advisable to have at least 2 extra for spares).
4 rolls of 3660mm x 610mm x 50mm ceramic blanket.

Ironwork:
(The following are approximate sizes. Actual sizes should be measured from the kiln.)

8 1500mm tie rods (with nuts and washers to fit) for kiln.
8 560mm tie rods (with nuts and washers to fit) for lower chimney.
4 2210mm x 50mm corner angle-irons for kiln.
4 2210mm x 50mm corner angle-irons for lower part of the chimney.
4 50mm corner angle-irons for upper part of the chimney plus 8 tie bars.
2 1150mm x 75mm angle-iron thrust bars.
Sufficient iron to make up firebox doors.

Gas kiln

Approximate list of materials used:

18 Concrete blocks.
270 Firebricks.
220 Insulating bricks.
46 side arch bricks.
Common house bricks, enough to take the chimney up higher if required.
6 Firebars (advisable to have at least 2 extra for spares).
3 rolls of 3660mm x 610mm x 50mm ceramic blanket.

Ironwork:
(The following are approximate sizes. Actual sizes should be measured from the kiln.)

4 1100mm tie rods (with nuts and washers to fit) for kiln.
4 975mm tie rods (with nuts and washers to fit) for kiln.
8 520mm tie rods (with nuts and washers to fit) for chimney.
4 1600mm x 50mm corner angle-irons for kiln.
4 2000mm x 50mm corner angle-irons for chimney.
2 900mm x 75mm angle-iron thrust bars.
Sufficient iron to make up firebox doors.

List of Suppliers

UK

SUPPLIERS OF KILN MATERIALS

Acme Batt Co.
(*Kiln props and shelves*)
Walter Brayford
Grove Cottage
Clay Lake
Endon
Stoke-on-Trent
ST9 9DE
Tel: 01782 505405
E-mail: walter@claylake.com

DSF Refractories & Minerals Ltd
(*Firebricks, insulating bricks and ceramic fibre*)
Friden, Newhaven
Nr. Buxton
Derbyshire
SK17 0DX
Tel: 01629 636271
E-mail: info@dsf.co.uk

Hot Box Ltd
(*Firebricks, insulating bricks and ceramic fibre*)
53 Newcastle Street
Burslem
Stoke-on-Trent
ST3 3QP
Tel: 01782 835666

IMS
(*Firebricks, insulating bricks and ceramic fibre*)
Bridge Street
Wordsley
Stourbridge
West Midlands
DY8 5YU
Tel: 01384 76493

Kitsons Thermal Supplies
(*Firebricks, insulating bricks, ceramic fibre and many other refractory products*)
(Branches all over the UK)
London West (Ruislip) Branch
Victoria Road Retail Park
Crown Road
Ruislip
HA4 0AF
Tel: 020 8839 4290
Email:
ruislip@kitsonsthermal.co.uk
www.kitsonsthermal.co.uk

S.B.S Engineering
(*Pyrometers*)
Ty Newydd
Horeb
Llandysul
SA44 4JG
Tel: 01559 363708
E-mail:
sbstempcontrol@hotmail.com

Stedmark Ltd
(*Gas burners*)
Unit 11, Derby Road Industrial Estate
Heanor
Derbyshire
DE75 7QL
Tel: 01773 713300
E-mail: sales@stedmark.com

Studweld Pro (SWP) Refractory Bricks
(*Firebricks, insulating bricks and ceramic fibre*)
Ollerton Road
Nr. Newark
Nottinghamshire
NG22 0PQ
Tel: 01777 874500

Yorkshire Refractory Products Limited
(*Firebricks, insulating bricks and ceramic fibre*)
Unit 9, Leebridge Ind. Est
Leebridge Road
Halifax
West Yorkshire
HX3 5HE
Tel: 01422 353344
E-mail: sales@yrpl.com
Web: www.yrpl.com

GENERAL SUPPLIERS

Bath Potters Supplies
Unit 18, Forth Avenue
Westfield Trading Estate
Radstock

BA3 4XE
Tel: 01761 411077
www.bathpotters.demon.co.uk

Potclays Ltd
Brick Kiln Lane
Etruria, Stoke-on-Trent
Staffordshire
ST4 7BP
Tel: 01782 219816
www.potclays.co.uk

Potterycrafts Ltd
Campbell Road
Stoke-on-Trent
Staffordshire ST4 4ET
Tel: 01782 745000
www.potterycrafts.co.uk

North America

SUPPLIERS OF KILN MATERIALS

Aardvark Clay & Supplies Inc.
(*Supply most kiln building equipment*)
1400 E. Pomona Street
Santa Ana
CA 92705-4812
Tel: 714 541 4157
Fax: 714 541 2021
www.aardvarkclay.com

Aardvark Clay & Supplies Inc.
(2nd branch)
(*Supply most kiln building equipment*)
6230 Greyhound Lane, Suite E
Las Vegas
NV 89122 7625
Tel: 702 451 9898
www.aardvarkclay.com

Axner Pottery Supply
(*Pyrometers, burners, shelves & insulation*)
P.O. Box 621484
Oviedo FL 32762-1484
E-mail: axner@axner.com
Website: www.axner.com

Bailey Ceramic Supply
(*Pyrometers, shelves, bricks & insulation)*
P.O. Box 1577
62 Tenbroeck Avenue
Kingston
NY 12402
Tel: 845 339 3721
www.baileypottery.com

Continental Clay Company
(*Pyrometers, shelves & insulation)*
1101 Stinson Blvd NE
Minneapolis
MN 55413
Tel: 612 331 9332
www.continentalclay.com

Refractories West Inc.
(Refractories, castables, insulating materials, shelves, high alumina & fireclay bricks)
33163 Braniff Ave
Pueblo, Colorado 81001
Tel: 719 544 9043
www.refwest.com

GENERAL SUPPLIERS

Atlantic Pottery Supplies
15 Canal Street
Dartmouth
Nova Scotia
B2Y 2W19
Tel: 902 466 6947
www.atlanticpottery.com

East Bay Clay
200 South First Street
Richmond
CA 94804
Tel: 510 233 1800

Laguna Clay Company
1440 Lomitas Avenue
City of Industry
CA 91746
Tel: 800 452 4862
www.lagunaclay.com

Leslie Ceramics Supply Company
1212 San Pablo Avenue
Berkeley
CA 94706
Tel: 510 524 7363
www.leslieceramics.com

Mile Hi Ceramics
77 Lipan, Denver
Colorado
80223-1580
Tel: 303 825 4570
www.milehiceramics.com

Plainsman Clays Ltd
Box 1266
702 Wood Street
Medicine Hat
Alberta
T1A 7M9
Tel: 403 527 8535
www.plainsmanclays.com

Glossary

Arch former Temporary structure to support a brick arch while it is being built.

Cones Pyrometric cones are made from ceramic materials, to calculated formula, that will bend and melt at given temperatures. They are placed within the kiln where they can be seen through a spy-hole. Similar in composition to glazes, they give a more accurate indication of the heatwork on the ware than a temperature reading from a pyrometer.

Damper A device for adjusting the exit flue or chimney.

Drip-plate Made from thick metal, sometimes formed in a louver shape. Oil and water dripped onto the hot metal creates a fierce flame.

Fail-safe device A device fitted to a gas burner that will cut off the gas supply should the flame go out.

Flue The channel where smoke, hot gases or flames travel through and out of the kiln.

Flux An oxide within the glaze or clay, which encourages melting by interacting with other oxides.

Oxidation – The process where excess air is introduced to the fire to give a 'clean' atmosphere within the kiln. Its importance in pottery is to burn-off, by oxidising, injurious volatiles contained within the clay and glaze.

Passive damper Places in the exit flue or chimney where loose bricks can be taken out, so allowing air from outside the kiln to be drawn up the chimney, thus decreasing the speed of the exiting hot gases.

Raku A low-fired glazed pottery by a direct process which involves placing the pots, with the unfired glaze, into a red-hot kiln and taking them straight out when the glaze has melted. First produced in Japan in the 16th century.

Reduction The action of taking oxygen away from the metal oxides in the glaze and clay during the firing process. This is achieved by adding more fuel or reducing the available air to the firebox.

Skewback A shaped brick that sits on the top of the chamber wall that transfers the weight of the arch through to the wall.

Soaking The action of holding the temperature at any point during the firing. It is most often used at around 1000°C (1832°F), to help burn-off unwanted volatiles, and at the end of a firing to allow the temperature within the kiln to even out.

Soda port An opening in the kiln, usually a loose brick that can be removed when needed, to allow a soda solution to be sprayed into the kiln.

Springer See 'skewback'.

Thrust bars A strong metal bar, usually made from angle-iron or channel-iron that supports the chamber wall at the point where the skewback bricks are laid.

Wicket The entry hole or doorway into the kiln chamber.

Bibliography

Cardew, Michael, *Pioneer Pottery*, A&C Black Publishers Ltd (London) and The American Ceramic Society (Ohio), 2002

Gregory, Ian, *Kiln Building*, second edition, A&C Black Publishers Ltd (London), 2001

Gregory, Ian, *Alternative Kilns*, A&C Black Publishers Ltd (London) and University of Pennsylvania Press (Philadelphia), 2005

Hamer, Frank and Janet, *The Potter's Dictionary of Materials and Techniques*, fifth edition, A&C Black Publishers Ltd (London) and University of Pennsylvania Press (Philadelphia), 2004

Lou, Nils, *The Art of Firing*, A&C Black Publishers Ltd (London) and Gentle Breeze Publishing (Florida), 1998

Norsker, Henrik, *Refractories and Kilns for the Self-Reliant Potter*, 2nd edition, Friedr. Vieweg & Sohn Verlagsgesellschaft mbH, Braunschweig, 1999

Olsen, Frederick L. *The Kiln Book*, second edition, A&C Black Publishers Ltd (London), 1983

Rhodes, Daniel, *Kilns, Design, Construction and Operation*, Pitman and Sons Ltd (London), 1969

Websites

www.joefinchkilns.co.uk
www.ukpotters.co.uk
www.ceramicstoday.com
www.studiopottery.co.uk
www.olsenkilns.com
www.mudslinger.demon.co.uk

Index